Don't Pay Too Much Tax if You're Employed

PERSONAL FINANCE GUIDES

In the same series:

Don't Pay Too Much Tax If You're Self–Employed
David Williams

Running Your Own Business
David Williams

Making the Most of Your Money
Helen Pridham

Don't Pay Too Much Tax if You're Employed

David Williams

NICHOLAS BREALEY

PUBLISHING

LONDON

First published in Great Britain by
Nicholas Brealey Publishing Limited in 1995
21 Bloomsbury Way
London WC1A 2TH

ISBN 1 85788 090 0

British Library Cataloguing-in-Publication Data
A catalogue record for this book is available from the British Library.

Every care has been taken in preparing this book.The guidance it contains is
sound at the time of publication but is not intended to be a substitute for
skilled professional assistance except in the most straightforward situations.
Because of this the author, the publishers and Allied Dunbar Assurance plc
(or any other company within the Allied Dunbar Group) can take no
responsibility for the outcome of action taken or not taken as a result of this
book.

The views and opinions of Allied Dunbar may not necessarily coincide with
some of the views and opinions expressed in this book which are solely
those of the author and no endorsement of them by Allied Dunbar should be
inferred.

The material herein which is Crown Copyright is reproduced with the
permission of the Controller of Her Majesty's Stationery Office.

Produced by Frere Publishing Services, 2 Whitehorse Street, London W1
Printed and bound in Finland by WSOY

Contents

Acknowledgements

This book, like its predecessors, is at the same time both my work and the work of many people. I am very pleased again to thank those who, knowingly or otherwise, helped with the ideas, information and technical expertise that helped put this book together. This is particularly true of Nicholas Brealey and Rupert Scott for their counsel and technical assistance in production. My thanks also to Lis, Ed and Tom for their forbearance. But, for all the help, the mistakes and omissions are mine.

I must also add two words of warning that apply to every tax book ever written. First, a book like this can give general guidance only. It cannot answer specific questions about difficult individual tax problems. Second, books on taxation date fast - every year something changes. However, this takes account of the announcements in the Budget for 1995-96, and all details announced up to January 1995.

David Williams

Introduction

You may think tax is bad news, or good news. But you will probably agree that it is a bad thing if you pay more tax than someone earning the same as you earn. Yet any system that leaves you and me with choices - for example, whether we have pensions or company cars - also leaves you and me paying different tax bills on similar income. That is partly because some people claim allowances and advantages due to them and some do not. This book aims to explain to you how this might be. It is not about policies or politicians. Rather, it is about one of the most complex areas of our law and the one which most of us have to comply with most of the time.

There's a lot of tax about. Maybe it doesn't sound much, but 25% on this and 10% of that add up. That is why it is important to understand the taxes that you pay when you earn anything. Hopefully, by understanding how tax is collected from you and all other employees, you will have a clearer idea about how much tax you need to pay ... and how much you don't have to pay. If I may repeat what I said in my companion book, *Don't Pay Too Much Tax If You're Self-Employed*, you owe it to yourself to understand your taxes. Otherwise, who knows what you will owe to others?

1   *Plucking the geese!*

HOW MUCH TAX DO YOU PAY?

*T*he answer that many politicians have given privately is, unfortunately, "as much as we can get them to pay before they start complaining." What has that to do with geese? One of the more honest tax-gatherers once said :

> *The art of taxation consists in so plucking the goose as to obtain the largest amount of feathers with the least possible amount of hissing.*

That individual should have known. He was treasurer to the French king who, among other little ventures, built the palace at Versailles!

In the last few years, taxpayers have become rather better at hissing. Remember the poll tax, and the proposal to raise VAT on fuel to the full rate? But taxes will never go away and - whatever politicians are prone to say - are in total higher today than in many peacetime years past.

However, despite the threat of hissing, many people end up paying more tax than they need, because they do not know how much they pay and how much they need to pay.

Do you know how much tax you pay in a year? Probably not. If you are working, how much tax will you pay if you earn an extra £? The answer is probably over 30%. Why?

CHECK YOUR
PAY CHEQUE

Because you are paying both income tax and NI contributions on that £. The basic rate of income tax (which is what most people pay) is 25%. The main rate of Class 1 NI contributions (which is, again, what most people pay) is 10%. In addition, the employer may be paying a further 10% employers' contribution.

In other words, for the employer to pay you £100, the employer may be paying out over £110. Of that you see £65. Added up that way, the tax on your extra pound can come to over 40%. That's so even though the higher rate of income tax is just 40%.

Do you know how much you will pay in income tax and NI contributions this year? Are you paying the right amount?

Did you take any notice when you received your last P 60 (the form that told you how much tax you paid last year)? Did you understand it? Did you pay too much? Have you claimed any deductions to which you are entitled? If not, what can you do about it?

The purpose of this book is to help you understand how and when you have to pay tax on your earnings, and when you don't have to pay. It looks at the two taxes paid by you and your employer on your earnings:

THE PURPOSE OF
THIS BOOK

Income Tax, which is normally paid for you through PAYE (Pay As You Earn), and

National Insurance (NI for short)

contributions paid by both you and your employer, but also collected through PAYE.

WHAT THIS BOOK COVERS

In this chapter we look at how you pay tax on your earnings, and the role played by the two tax departments involved in the process. We also look at what happens if you have paid too much tax or too little tax. We are assuming that you are an employee. This is not always clear, and in the next chapter we outline the problems. However, this book does not cover tax for the self-employed. That is dealt with fully in my other book, *Don't Pay Too Much Tax if You're Self-Employed.*

But how do you know how much tax you have paid? To find that out, we must look at all the ways people are paid, and find out how each of them is taxed. That is the theme of the main part of this book. The following chapters deal with cash payments, and then benefits in kind. Cars and share schemes, the most important of these kinds of benefits apart from pensions, are dealt with separately, then we cover all other kinds of benefits.

After that we look at the deductions you can claim from your income tax or that can be taken from your pay. Finally, we tackle pensions: both the payments you make into them and the benefits you get from them, with particular reference of course to how they are taxed, or not taxed. For most people pensions are the best ways both to save and to save tax, so this needs a close look.

IT'S GONE BEFORE YOU GET IT

For many years, the tax system on employees has been designed to do the work for them. Tax (and NI contributions) is taken from you by

PAYE each time you get paid. PAYE means "Pay As You Earn" although it might be better to call it "PAYGP" or pay as you get paid. You never see the tax, because it goes straight to the Revenue from your employer. At the same time, neither the Revenue nor your employer is required to explain why you have to pay the tax you do. This book aims to do that. It also aims to show you the different ways people are paid, and how these different ways are taxed.

If your employer follows the procedures correctly in collecting tax from you through PAYE, you will probably pay roughly the right amount of tax on the cash you receive. It's not so easy with other benefits, such as the company car. Nor is it obvious why, for example, taking part in a company share scheme is a good idea. We will look at each of those.

Under the PAYE system, you have to do very little. Most years, you will not be asked to fill in any forms, or make any direct payments. This is because your employer and the tax authorities will do all the work for you. There are formalities you must follow when starting or changing jobs, but these are not major problems. Nearly everyone who is an employer is required to operate PAYE. The only exceptions are those whose employees all earn below the weekly amounts on which tax and NI contributions start to be paid. In 1995/96, any employer taking on someone for £58 a week or more is obliged to tell the tax authorities of the fact. Once notified, the tax authorities will direct the employer to collect tax and NI contributions from the pay in the correct manner.

Who are the tax authorities? There are two that get involved in taxing pay, the Inland Revenue and the Contributions Agency.

WHO DOES
WHAT IN TAX

THE INLAND REVENUE

The Inland Revenue, or Revenue, is responsible for income tax. It is known officially as the Board of Inland Revenue, and its senior officers are the Commissioners of Inland Revenue. The Inland Revenue is a government department, although it is not run by a minister. Instead, the Treasury Ministers keep an eye on it. This arrangement is important, because the Revenue keeps itself totally independent of politics. Its headquarters is at Somerset House on the Strand in central London.

The Revenue is represented locally by a tax office headed by inspectors of tax. As an employee, you will have little to do with them, unless you want some information or have other forms of income.

If you want to raise a problem with them, you will be best dealing with the tax office responsible for your employer's payroll. If you work for a large employer, this will probably not be your local tax office. Instead, it may be a PAYE office that may be at the other end of the country. For example, your employer might be monitored through a London Provincial Office, which might be in Scotland. This is particularly true for big companies with centralised payrolls although the employees are based all over the country. Your employer's finance department will tell you where it is. However, you can make general enquiries at your local office, or by checking if there is an enquiry office locally in your phone book.

Tax offices have a wide range of leaflets about the special rules for income tax. Some are mentioned in this book. If you are interested, ask the local tax office for a copy. They are all free. If you have problems, you should also contact the tax office. They have adopted the Taxpayer's Charter, under which you should be offered help and advice. This is set out in the box opposite.

THE TAXPAYER'S CHARTER

You are entitled to expect the Inland Revenue

To be fair
- By settling your tax affairs impartially
- By expecting you to pay only what is due under the law
- By treating everyone with equal fairness

To help you
- To get your tax affairs right
- To understand your rights and obligations
- By providing clear leaflets and forms
- By giving you information and assistance at our enquiry offices
- By being courteous at all times

To provide an efficient service
- By settling your tax affairs promptly and accurately
- By keeping your private affairs strictly confidential
- By using the information given us only as allowed by the law
- By keeping to a minimum your costs of complying with the law
- By keeping our costs down

To be accountable for what we do
- By setting standards for ourselves and publishing how well we live up to them

If you are not satisfied
- We will tell you exactly how to complain
- You can ask for your tax affairs to be looked at again
- You can appeal to an independent tribunal
- Your MP can refer your complaint to the Ombudsman

In return, we need you
- To be honest
- To give us accurate information
- To pay your tax on time

THE CONTRIBUTIONS AGENCY

The Contributions Agency may be a new name to you. It is an agency within the DSS or Department of Social Security.

This means that it is still part of the Department of Social Security but it is run as a separate organisation within the DSS, with its own executive head. In reality, the Agency is a new name and organisation that is now doing a job long done by the same staff as DSS officers. However, the Agency now has direct responsibility for all aspects of collecting and maintaining records of contributions from its headquarters at Newcastle upon Tyne.

The Agency does not have its own local offices. Instead, you will find the Agency staff working as part of the local Social Security Offices. There they work alongside the staff of the Benefits Agency. That is another part of the DSS, responsible for paying social security benefits. Indeed, the same staff may deal with contributions and also deal with the contributory benefits such as retirement pensions and invalidity benefit.

You are also unlikely to have direct dealings with the Contributions Agency as a contributor, at least if you don't claim a contributory benefit, in most years.

NI contributions (short for National Insurance contributions) will be collected by your employer and paid to the Revenue along with your tax. The Revenue then pays them to the Agency for you.

The Agency has a Contributor's Charter similar to the taxpayer's charter, so we do not repeat it here. But, like the Revenue, the Agency publishes free leaflets on key points, and will help you if you have a problem.

The Revenue and the Contributions Agency are separate bodies. This is because income tax and NI contributions, although collected together, are separate payments for separate purposes.

Income tax is a general tax, paid to the government in the same way as other general taxes such as VAT or the tax on tobacco. NI contributions are paid into a separate national account, the National Insurance Fund, apart from a small part that is put towards the cost of the national health service. The National Insurance Fund is used to pay for the main social security contributory benefits. Most of it goes towards funding retirement pensions, and the balance to other benefits such as unemployment benefit. The National Insurance Fund does not pay for the "safety net" benefits such as income support or family credit.

Because NI contributions are paid towards benefit, each contribution made by someone in employment is counted towards the benefit entitlement of the employee paying it. Full state retirement pension can only be claimed by those with a good contribution record over their working lives.

The main contributory benefits are: retirement pension (including earnings-related supplement), widow's benefits, unemployment benefit, and incapacity benefit. Most other benefits are financed out of general taxation.

This book does not discuss social security benefits, except for brief mentions of benefits in suitable places. Booklets and leaflets describing benefits can be obtained free of charge from local social security offices and most local post offices. You can obtain help for an individual problem by phoning the DSS Helpline on 0800 666 555. They will also deal with straightforward queries about contributions.

I CAN'T UNDERSTAND IT

Some of our tax laws are complicated and extremely difficult to understand - even for the experts. There are several reasons for this. One is that parts of the laws were first written nearly 200 years ago, and have never been properly updated. Another is that they aim to deal with every case fairly (and that, with millions of taxpayers, means lots of rules). Another is the fact that the laws result from endless battles between tax collectors and tax avoiders. Good laws are rarely simple laws. Fair tax laws are rarely short laws. Some complication is therefore a good thing - but not all of it!

In recent years, determined attempts have been made to simplify some of the rules. For example, government ministers have announced that some of the rules of income tax are being looked at again to see what can be removed.

The result is a law that is easier to explain now than in the 1980s.

The tax authorities are also much better than they used to be some years ago at publishing guidance, and discussing problems.

Despite the complication, the underlying tax rules are usually quite simple. It is those rules that we emphasise as we go along.

We will also, as we go, debug some of the jargon that surrounds tax. Hopefully, if we can cut some of the jargon, you can see if you can cut some of the tax.

If you find through this book that you are paying more taxes than you need to, you are entitled to reduce them. This is the first principle of tax that we should note:

You are required to pay only the taxes that the tax authorities are clearly authorised to collect.

For example, for NI purposes if you receive a benefit in kind, then there are no NI contributions to pay. But if you receive the money from your employer to buy the same item, there will be NI contributions on the cash. You are free, with your employer, to choose how you are paid. There is nothing to stop you therefore being paid in kind rather than cash, even though this saves money. (It also may lose you some benefit entitlement, but that is part of your choice too.)

There is, however, an important practical rule that is found in all our taxes. As between the tax authorities and the taxpayers, it is for taxpayers to show that tax authorities are wrong, and not the other way round. More formally, the burden of proof in establishing a question of fact is on the taxpayer. If you claim some expense, or that something is not work-related, it is for you to show the tax staff that it is so.

CAN I CUT MY TAXES?

It is always up to you to claim any allowances or deductions, such as expenses. Another basic rule of our tax laws is that **you are not entitled to any deduction or allowance unless the law contains clear authority for it.** Just because you spend something on your job does not mean you can get a tax deduction for it.

Further, you will not normally be allowed any deduction or allowance unless you claim it. For

CLAIMING DEDUCTIONS

example, you find, having read this book, that you should be claiming something for your car. It is up to you to tell your tax office that. The tax office to tell is the one that does the PAYE at your place of work. It will also be for you to prove that you have actually spent the money you say you spent. For that, you will need receipts or other proof if you are asked for it.

E & OE?

Errors and omissions excepted? No.

What happens if you find that you could have claimed an allowance last year as well as this year, and you have done neither. Can you deal with the error? Yes.

OVERPAID TAX

Although tax bills are usually settled on a yearly basis, they can be corrected for up to six years back. For example, you find that, due to an error, you have been paying too much tax in June 1995. You can claim for that error to be corrected not only in that tax year, but the six previous years as well. This would take you back to 1989. Of course, you will need to be able to prove the error goes back that far.

So, if you find that your tax has not been worked out right, and you are the loser, you can ask for a correction for earlier years as well. But you cannot go back further than six years.

UNDERPAID TAX

The six year rule applies to both taxpayers and the tax authorities. They can also go back six years to claim underpaid tax. If they find that someone has failed to pay tax on income, they may impose an assessment on the taxpayer for tax for the current year and each of the previous six years. They can also impose an interest charge, and can add penalties if the taxpayer has not been complying with his or her legal duties.

Sometimes an employer fails to pay PAYE tax to the Revenue, even though it has been collected from the employee. All employers have between one month and three months to collect tax before they pay it to the tax office. If during that period something happens, then the tax may never be paid. This happens, for instance, where a business goes bankrupt after collecting tax from employees.

In other cases, the employer may deliberately or because of a mistake collect too much tax, too little tax, or no tax at all from an employee. Tax officers and officers of the Contributions Agency visit employers to check if they are carrying out their duties right. A visit from an officer may help put the mistakes right. But what if the employee maintains tax has already been paid? Are the employees liable to pay the underpaid tax, or pay over to the tax authorities tax already paid to the employer?

If an employer has deducted too little tax from an employee, the employer can be made to pay the tax as if it had been deducted. Often such settlements will be made without reference to individual employees, but will cover the tax collectable by the employer generally. If the tax officer is satisfied that the employer has made a genuine mistake in underdeducting tax, and that the employer was taking reasonable care to operate the PAYE system properly, then the employee, and not the employer, can be required to pay the amount underpaid.

If the employer has deliberately undercollected

tax, and the employee knows this, then the employee can again be made liable for the underpaid tax. In this sort of case, the employee can also be made to pay interest and penalties on the underpayment. For example, in a small firm the directors agree to underdeclare the tax. As a result, the business does not deduct enough tax. In that case these powers could be used to ensure that the directors did pay the right tax.

If an employee has paid tax to the employer, he or she cannot usually be made to pay it again to the tax authorities.

DISPUTES

In some cases, a disagreement might arise about whether the employee had or had not paid the right amount of tax. Such cases do not happen very often. If they do, there is a little known appeal right open to the employee. This is the right to take the dispute to the income tax appeal tribunal. The tribunal, known under its official title as the General Commissioners, has the power to decide which of the employer and employee is right. It will do so after an independent hearing of the case.

An employee who wishes to challenge the employer's decision in this way should seek advice. This could be obtained from a union, a citizen's advice bureau or a professional tax adviser before taking a course such as this. In the last resort, an aggrieved employee would need to refer the matter to her or his local tax office, to get the matter brought up before the Commissioners. Their decision is final.

2   *Being an employee*

... if you are. In several areas of the service industry there have been running arguments between the tax authorities and taxpayers for years over whether someone is or is not an employee. This applies particularly to part-time workers, and those working flexitime. Both are of course growing in importance as groups of workers within the job market.

WHY DOES IT MATTER?

Why does it matter whether you are an employee or not? The main reason is that PAYE has to be applied to the pay of almost all employees. This means that tax has to be deducted at source by the employer. The self-employed pay tax later, when they make their tax returns. The tax authorities prefer people to be employees for this reason. It is easier for them, and they are more likely to collect the tax.

A second reason is that employees have to pay Class 1 National Insurance contributions (or NICs as they are increasingly called), and so do their employers. That may involve both employees and their employers paying 10% of earnings every time the employees are paid. (See table on page 57 for details.)

The self-employed usually pay a lower amount. However, the self-employed get less by way of social security benefits than employees.

A third reason is that employees can only claim limited work expenses against their tax. A self-employed person has much greater scope for claiming expenses. For example, a self-employed person can claim for use of part of the home as an office. Again, however, the self-employed do not always come off best. In some cases, where employees are being paid in kind by their employers the tax treatment is better than that for the self-employed.

A self-employed person may have to register for VAT. Employees never do. That is the problem of their employer. (For this reason, we do not discuss VAT in this book.)

BEING A COMPANY

People who set up one-person companies can sometimes get the best (or worst) of both worlds. For example, Jo is running a successful small business making and selling widgets. Jo decides to turn the business into a company, Jo Ltd, becoming sole holder of the shares in the company, and also its main director. Setting up a company is easy to do (and may only cost about £100). But it makes fundamental changes to the tax position. When Jo was running the business as an individual, she was self-employed. Now the company runs the business, she is a director and probably an employee also. In addition she is the shareholder. So, instead of receiving profits as a self-employed person she receives earnings as an employee. The fees received by a director are treated in the same way as employees, so it will make little difference from a tax standpoint whether she has a salary or not. She may also receive dividends as owner.

This is because the company, Jo Ltd, is, of course, in business on its own. Payments to the company cannot be subject to PAYE. Jo, although the sole owner, director, and employee of the company is not running the business directly. However, she can clearly arrange to be paid by the company in the most tax-efficient way. Tax will not always be avoided by loans, rather than earnings, but profits could be paid out as dividends instead, or saved within the company. In this way, in a practical sense the person is in a similar position to the self-employed while undoubtedly an employee in law.

ARE YOU AN EMPLOYEE?

This book explores and explains all these issues, and many more. Throughout, it is concerned with the position of the employee. We do not discuss matters of concern only to the self-employed such as VAT and trading tax. This is because I have already written a companion book covering these, *Don't Pay Too Much Tax if You're Self-Employed*.

At the end of this chapter we discuss the rules that decide if you are an employee. It is usually not a problem. If it is, read the end of the chapter first.

ONCE AN EMPLOYEE, ALWAYS AN EMPLOYEE?

No. A person who is an employee can become a self-employed person while working for the same paymaster, but only if the paymaster excludes the worker from the organisation and stops control over the worker's work.

Someone who is an employee can also be a self-employed person at the same time. Each job has to be looked at separately. The tax and NI rules will apply separately to each job or employment, except where the jobs are for the same or associated employers. There is, however, a maximum amount of NI contributions that an employee with more than one job can be required to pay.

WHAT MUST YOU PAY?

That's not a silly question. On the contrary, it's the whole purpose of the book to explain what has to be paid, and what does not have to be paid.

Employees must pay :

Income tax under Schedule E on all "emoluments" from all employments, and

Class 1 NI contributions from all "earnings" from all employments.

Employers must pay :
Class 1 NI contributions on all earnings of all employees
Class 1A NI contributions in respect of any company cars and free fuel provided to employees

---

WHO MUST PAY INCOME TAX?

Everyone. You pay income tax regardless of your age, your sex, whether you are married or not, your nationality or any other factor, if you have an income in the UK that is of a kind liable to income tax. All UK earnings are liable to income tax. And the same rates of tax apply to everyone. There are different rules for overseas earnings, and we outline these in a later chapter.

Income tax rates : 1995/96

The rates of income tax are :

The lower rate (on the first £3,200 of taxable income) :	20%
The standard rate (on the pay above £3,200 up to £24,300):	25%
The higher rate (on taxable pay over £24,300 a year):	40%

WHO MUST PAY NICS?

Only those who are either employed or self-employed, if they are of working age. The rates at which contributions are paid depend on whether someone is employed or self-employed, and the pension arrangements linked to their work. There are also other special rules, for example applying to some married women and widows. These special rules are outlined at the end of this chapter.

Even this brief outline shows that some people will pay income tax, but not NICs, while others will pay NICs but not income tax. Both must be checked separately. Nor, as we shall see next, are the rules the same as to the pay on which the tax and NICs are based.

EMOLUMENTS AND EARNINGS

As noted in the box, you will pay income tax on the total "emoluments" you receive from your employments, and your total "earnings" from them. Technically, "emoluments" and "earnings" are not the same thing. For example "earnings" do not include most benefits in kind, while "emoluments" do. This means that you do not pay income tax and NI contributions on the same amounts. Sometimes you will pay both, and sometimes only one. We explain the differences in detail in several of the chapters below. The differences can be very important, as the next example shows.

Nick's job

Nick is a member of staff at Workshop plc. He earns a regular salary, plus a profit-related bonus and some benefits in kind. His salary is £20,000 and is subject to both income tax and NICs. His bonus is liable to NICs but not income tax, and his benefits in kind are subject to income tax and not NICs.

On each £10 of his salary he and Workshop will pay tax and NICs as follows : Nick pays tax at 25% and NICs at 10%, a total of 35% or £3.50. This leaves £6.50 after deductions. Workshop pays an employers NIC on the salary at 10.2% or £1.02. So it costs them £11.02 to pay him £6.50

On each £10 of bonus, the NICs are payable but not the income tax. He therefore receives £9 of the bonus, but Workshop has to pay £11.02p.
So he is better off.

On each £10 worth of benefits in kind, the income tax is payable but not the NICs. So Workshop pays the £10, and Nick gets £7.50. Here they are both better off (except that Nick may lose out in the longer run by not having paid any contributions towards benefit entitlement).

Have you heard the word "emoluments" before? Probably not. It is not a word in everyday use. But it is the official word used in the tax law. Why do our tax laws use such odd words? This is partly because the tax law is nearly two hundred years old (it was first agreed by Parliament in 1803), and sometimes uses outdated language. "Schedule E" is another example of this. It is the official description for the rules that impose income tax on earnings from employments. Our tax laws are extremely

EMOLUMENTS

complicated, partly because officials and politicians are both extremely cautious about changing the words in a tax law. They may make an expensive mistake if they try to be too clever!

SCHEDULE E

The rules of what is called Schedule E are, in effect, a wages tax, but we do not call them that. We say that they are just one part of the one income tax. There are other special rules for income from trades, income from land, taxation of savings, taxation of companies and taxation of capital gains. They are in other "Schedules". Those rules are summarised in my book *Don't Pay Too Much Tax If You're Self-Employed*. Most employees pay tax only on their earnings and a small amount of tax on savings, and these are the rules on which we concentrate here.

HOW TO CUT TAX

There are only three ways that any tax bill can be reduced legally:

By changing how things happen so you turn something that is taxable into something that is not taxable, or into something that is taxable at a lower level

By setting off against taxable income all the deductions that are available to the taxpayer

By delaying the time that the tax is paid.

TAX AVOIDANCE

Any of these activities may be called tax planning or tax avoidance. There is nothing illegal about this. However, anyone attempting to cut their tax bills by, for example, deliberately misleading the tax authorities or pretending something has happened that did not happen is evading tax, not avoiding it. Their actions are illegal. There are stiff penalties for those caught evading tax. You do not hear of them very often. This is because the Inland Revenue, in particular, keeps the affairs of taxpayers quiet, and rarely uses the criminal courts. They collect many millions of pounds a year in penalties. You will not read about this in the papers. But it happens.

How do you cut taxes by tax planning? Look again at the example of Nick's job. This shows three different results from something worth £10 to Nick. If both income tax and NICs were avoided, we would have a fourth result - others again if we take account of the points about deductions and delays. The different rules produce a number of practical differences both in timing and cost, although in each case the taxpayers are complying fully with the law.

Many schemes, both simple and complicated, have developed to exploit these differences. Some may help the employer as much as the employee. Some of these schemes are not particularly popular with the tax authorities if they result in earnings that should be paid in cash being paid in other ways just to cut the tax bill. However, governments have actively encouraged some schemes because they believe them to be in the overall interest of all concerned. Here the tax or NIC savings are used to encourage and not to discourage the use of these schemes. The cut in taxes is a sort of bonus for dealing with things in the preferred way, for example receiving pay in the form of profit-related pay.

This leaves us with two important messages. First, provided that we comply with the law, it is our right to cut our taxes if we can. If that is not what the government or Parliament wants, they can always change the law. Second, the government sometimes encourages us to cut taxes. Cutting tax bills is not always a bad thing to them!

PAYE

One of the ways of cutting taxes is to delay payment. Employees cannot often do that. This is because the UK tax system contains rules which collect income tax from salaries and wages as they are paid. The rules also apply to NICs. The money is collected on behalf of the government by the employer. The employer must then pay that tax over to the tax authorities, usually every month. This is done through a clever scheme known as PAYE.

PAYE means "pay as you earn" (though the way it works might be described better as pay as you get paid). PAYE is the main way that both income tax on emoluments, and Class 1 NI contributions on earnings are collected. It is a complex but clever way in which the employer must deduct both income tax and NI contributions from your pay each time you are paid - unless you don't owe any tax or NICs at all.

The system is complex to deal with the fact that different people don't pay the same tax on the same earnings. This is because, as we examine in later chapters, they may have different deductions or allowances to claim against their tax liabilities. They are also entitled to personal allowances that differ between taxpayers.

PAYE takes all the differences into account by issuing everyone with a tax code. You should receive a notice of your current tax code from time to time on a formal *Notice of your income tax code* from your local Inspector of Taxes. The Inspector is the local official responsible for supervising the assessment of income tax. The form is also called form P2. If your tax code is right, then the employer should collect the right amount of income tax from you over the tax year.

Provided that the tax code is right, and the employer has made no mistake, PAYE will take from you each time you are paid enough tax and NICs to ensure that you pay the total due from you evenly over the year. When it works properly, and you have no other earnings, you will not need to fill in any forms or tax returns. Nor will the tax authorities need to take any formal action to collect any other tax from you, or even to check that you have paid the right amount. They may do this during the year by checks that your employer is working PAYE properly.

You do not need a tax code for NICs, because they are worked out differently. There are no allowable expenses for NICs, and no personal allowances. You pay NICs on your total earnings each time you receive them.

When you receive a tax code notice, you should check it. Otherwise you may end up paying too much tax, and may not realise this. The form tells you on the back what to do if you disagree - write to the tax office objecting, and explaining why. A leaflet, P3, which usually comes with the Tax Code notice, fully explains how tax codes work, and you should ask for a copy if you think there are problems and one was not sent to you. Your local Inspector of Taxes will send you one

TAX CODES

free if asked. Here are some helpful hints about checking the tax code.

CHECKING YOUR TAX CODE

The Tax code notice has two columns on it. The one on the left looks like this :

See note	Allowances	£
17	PERSONAL ALLOWANCE	3445
17	MARRIED ALLOWANCE	1720
26	TAXED PAYMENT	385
	Total allowances	5550

This column sets out all the deductions that the inspector has allowed against your income tax this year. In the example, there are two personal allowances, and a deduction for a charity payment made under a deed of covenant. The note numbers refer to paragraphs in the leaflet P3 which explain the allowances.

PERSONAL ALLOWANCES

Everyone is entitled to a personal allowance. This means that everyone is entitled to earn a certain amount of money before they start paying income tax. The example above includes two personal allowances (the second one is the married couple's allowance) and a deduction. Everyone is entitled to at least one personal allowance. The allowances are:

Personal allowance
everyone is entitled to a personal allowance. If you are over 65, the allowance is higher, and if you are over 75 it increases again. In the case of married or unmarried couples, both the partners are taxed separately, and both get their own personal allowance. It is not transferable, so a non-working wife

cannot get the allowance deducted from her husband's pay.

Married couple's allowance

this can be claimed by either the husband or wife of a married couple (not both). It cannot be claimed by unmarried couples. However, where unmarried couples are bringing up children (a quick test is if they are receiving child benefit for one or more children), then one of the couple can claim the same amount of allowance as one parent allowance. A widow can also claim a similar amount in the year her husband dies as a widow's bereavement allowance.

Blind person's allowance

available if the taxpayer (and the taxpayer's husband or wife, if not separately claimed) is registered blind. There are no personal allowances for any other kind of disability. They are dealt with only through the social security system, particularly the disability working allowance for low-paid workers who have disabilities.

The deductions are dealt with in later chapters.

The right side of the P2 tax code form contains another column. In many cases this may be blank, but it may look like this :

RESTRICTIONS ON ALLOWANCES

See note	Less amounts taken away to cover items shown below	£
29	UNPAID TAX £125	314
33	ALLCE RESTRICTION	344
	less total reductions	658
Net allowances - the amount of your pay or pension from which tax will not be deducted		4892

This column lists deductions from your allowances. In this example there are two. The first shows that the taxpayer owes some other tax, probably from a previous year (perhaps on savings or some other kind of income). For convenience, the tax code this year is being reduced so the taxpayer pays the arrears evenly over the year. That often suits taxpayers as well as the tax authorities.

The other deduction, the "allowance restriction" is because of the way personal allowances work. The main personal allowance is set against full taxable income. If you pay tax at 25%, you earn the amount of the allowance before paying tax at that rate. If you pay at 40%, the same thing happens (and the allowance is worth more in tax saved as a result). But the married couple's allowance and similar allowances are not set fully against tax. In 1995-96 a deduction is allowed against tax of only 15% of the allowance, whatever the tax rate paid by the individual. The allowance restriction therefore applies to reduce the effective amount of the allowance to stop too much tax being paid for it.

Right at the end of the notice is the tax code. In the case of the example, the tax code will look something like this :

489B or 489H or 489T.

The "489" is the value of the tax code (divided by 10). The letter indicates the kind of taxpayer : B for basic rate, H for higher rate, T for other cases, and there are other letters again for pensioners, and those subject to deduction without allowances (before the code has been calculated or where tax is imposed on a second job).

If the code number is too high or too low, you will not be paying the right amount of tax, and you should take it up with the tax office.

CHECKING WITH THE EMPLOYER

In most cases, the employer will be applying the PAYE coding correctly, although there may be the odd mistake. Mistakes and adjustments can be corrected as the tax year goes on, without any major problem, and they usually are. But what happens if the employer is not carrying out the PAYE rules properly. Say that the employer has not paid the tax over to the Inland Revenue. Can you be made to pay again, when you have already paid? What if the employer is deducting too much tax?

If the employer has taken tax from you, but failed to pay it to the tax authorities, you cannot normally be asked to pay again. Similarly, if the employer defaults in calculating the tax, that is not your fault. You can be made liable only if the employer has taken reasonable care in collecting tax under PAYE, and made a mistake in good faith, or if you receive earnings without tax deducted knowing that the employer has wilfully failed to deduct the tax that should have been deducted.

Where a dispute arises between an employer and an employee about the amount of tax deducted, and they cannot agree, the matter can be referred to the independent tax appeal commissioners. This rarely happens, but ask your local Tax Office if you feel you have a problem of this sort.

NI CONTRIBUTIONS

Along with income tax, you will also probably be paying NICs or NI contributions. Indeed, many people pay NICs but do not pay income tax. This is because the level at which people start paying NICs on their earnings is lower than the level at which they start paying income tax.

DON'T PAY TOO MUCH
NICS

Your employer will deduct NICs from your pay at the same time as income tax. Your tax code is not relevant to NICs, and the deduction system works in a very different way. This may mean that, if the employer has the wrong information about you, or if you have two or more jobs, you may end up paying too much NICs. Any error in payment of NICs is not adjusted automatically under the PAYE system, though any errors can be put right during the year. There are a number of special rules, and some groups do not have to pay NICs at all. In addition, many people do not pay at the full rate because they are contracted out. Check how NICs should apply to you.

WHO NEED NOT PAY
NICS?

We have already asked who must pay, and noted why it is important. The groups not liable to pay any NICs on their earnings are those :

Employees aged under 16: neither they nor their employers need pay any contributions.

Employees over 65 (men) or 60 (women) (regardless of whether they have retired or not), but the employer has to pay contributions.

Those who have previously been working overseas, and who are still covered by a foreign scheme. This usually happens where a person has been working in the UK for less than a year. (Special rules also apply to airline staff and ship crews because of time spent overseas.)

Those who have more than one job, who can avoid paying NICs on some of their jobs if they are paying their full share of NICs on other jobs.

Those who are treated by the rules as not having a job (discussed later in this chapter) or as being self-employed.

When pay is paid after a person dies, for example to the widow, no NICs are due (although income tax will be payable).

The main rate at which NICs are paid is called the standard rate. There are different standard rates for both employers and employees. The rates are set out and discussed in the next chapter. However, most people do not pay NICs at these standard rates, but at special rates. Special rates apply to :

PAYING NICS :
THE RATES

Contracted-out employees, who have occupational pensions or private pensions. They will be paying contributions to those pensions, and have to pay a lower level of NICs as a result. See the chapter on pensions. Most employees are contracted out.

Members of the armed forces, who pay slightly lower rates of NICs because they are entitled to a more limited range of NI benefits.

Some married women and widows. Those

who chose to do so in 1977, and who have not changed their minds, and remain married or widows (as the case may be), pay NICs at a reduced rate of 3.85%. Unless they are low earners, this will reduce the NICs paid, but also reduces entitlement to benefit. Any woman who started work after 1977 will be treated in exactly the same way as all men, except that, for the time being, their retirement age is assumed for contributions purposes to be 60 not 65.

WHO IS AN EMPLOYEE?

Before we get immersed in the tax details, we need first to look at what makes someone an employee. This vitally important decision should be easy to explain, but it is not. The issue of whether someone is an employee is important for several reasons. It is, as we have seen, fundamental to liability to income tax and NI contribution liability. It is equally important for liability to VAT. And it is also central to questions of entitlement to social security and pensions, to redundancy and unfair dismissal, to questions about contracts of employment, to health and safety legislation, and to liability in cases of accidents, and the duty to insure.

Despite its importance, there is no short or easy way to define or describe whether someone is or is not an employee. The technical definition is the same for all the taxes and all the other points we have raised. It is a question of law that has been evolved by the courts. Just to confuse things further, different courts at different times have decided the question with different emphases on what matters. It is because of this lack of clarity that the disputes between tax authorities and taxpayers have occurred.

One point is clear. If you are an employee, then this applies to all aspects of the law. You cannot claim to be self-employed for tax and NI purposes, and expect sympathy from the courts if you later claim to be an employee so as to get redundancy pay.

In one case where two workers tried this, they were found by the court to be employees, and obtained compensation for unfair dismissal. They had previously claimed to be self-employed, and had paid income tax and NICs on that basis. The court drew attention to this, and to the fact that their tax and NI bills would need recalculating to take account of the court ruling. In the result, the arrears of underpaid income tax and NI then due from them were almost certainly greater than the compensation, so they lost out in the end. And that did not take account of the lawyers' bills.

A second key point is that the description you give yourself does not decide the issue. Some employers are keen to sign contracts with those working for them stating clearly that their employees are "self-employed" and are themselves individually responsible for income tax, NI contributions, sick pay and so forth. Yet in all other ways their "self-employed staff" are treated like employees - required to be at work at a set place at a set time for set hours and following the manager's or chargehand's instructions.

If the status of the staff is disputed, the decision whether the staff in these cases are self-employed is not exclusively for them or the other party to the contract. It is for the authorities and the courts. A court might well decide in this case that the terms of the contract were misleading

AN EMPLOYEE FOR ALL REASONS

IS THERE A CONTRACT?

and wrong, and that the workers were really employees, so that the employer is required to pay tax and NI contributions for them. However, where there is a written contract it will be the terms of that document that decide the "true" relationship - all the terms, not just the names given to jobs.

If there is no contract at all, then the individual cannot be an employee. For example, if you work for someone for no reward at all and receive no benefits at all, you cannot be an employee. This is the status of those on Work Experience. Often, of course, there will be no written contract (even if there should be one), but the two parties have reached a verbal agreement. In these cases, the decision whether someone is an employee depends on looking at the whole relationship between the two sides.

WHO IS IN CHARGE?

The example in the previous paragraph illustrates one of the key elements of being an employee. It is that one person is under someone else's control. Whether he or she is a part-time shift-worker on a production line or a consultant surgeon, if the work is essentially controlled by someone else who pays the person doing the job for the work, the person doing the job is probably an employee.

This element of control may seem obvious where someone works for only one other person. If there is any doubt, think of the answers to the questions that follow. Could the individual also work for other people without asking for permission? Who decides when or where the work is done? Who decides the way in which the work is done ? Is the employee part and parcel of the employer's business organisation, or doing her or his own thing?

Does the worker have to turn up to do the work personally, or can someone else be sent along to do the work (the "employee's" employee?)? Who has the right to hire and fire?

Another way of looking at it is to ask if the individual is in business on his or her own? If the worker needs a truck, tools or a computer for the work, who provides it? How is payment made? Is the pay hourly, weekly, or by reference to particular contracts or work done? Is the person paying concerned whether the worker makes a profit or a loss?

IN BUSINESS ON YOUR OWN ACCOUNT

Those truly in business on their own are in charge of their own fate, and sink or swim by themselves.

DIRECTORS AND OFFICE HOLDERS

A large group of people who are not employees are treated as employees for tax and NIC purposes. There are people who are "office holders". All directors of companies come within this group. There are about 700,000 directors in the UK. They control their companies, and may have contracts of employment at the same time. Even if they do not, they are caught within PAYE. This applies also to those receiving earnings from other offices, such as trustees, auditors, paid officers of churches including the clergy, public officials such as judges, and MPs, councillors and other elected office holders. They are all to varying degrees independent of those that pay them, but are treated as employees for tax purposes by law.

SPECIAL NI RULES FOR EMPLOYEES

For most purposes, the rules about who is an employee and who is self-employed apply to NICs and social security benefits as they do to income tax. But there are some special rules, called Categorisation Regulations that provide some special rules for some people for NI purposes. In these cases, the income tax and NI treatment may vary. There are also some narrower special rules for income tax.

AGENCY WORKERS

A major group caught by the special rules are agency workers - whether cleaners, temps or other office workers, or actors, models or other performers. In most cases, agency workers are treated as being employed by their agencies whatever the actual arrangements between the agency, the worker and the person contracting for the services. This applies for both NI and income tax.

WORK WITHIN THE FAMILY

Special NI rules also apply to work within the family. If one of a married couple, say the husband, employs his wife to work for him in connection with his own work, the wife is treated as being the husband's employee. If the husband "employs" the wife to do the housework (or she employs him), then the rule is that there is no employment in law for NI purposes.

This reflects a general legal position that such deals are not regarded as enforceable contracts, and on this basis when a husband pays his wife, or vice versa, it might be ignored for income tax too, unless they both draw it to the attention of the tax authorities. This general approach, and the special NI rules, also apply where other members of a family employ each other to work within the home, save where there is a trade or business going on. For example, if the grandparents employ the grandchildren, this does not count at all.

Another special NI rule treats part-time teachers and lecturers as employees if they work for the same person more than three times in any three months. The effect of this rule is to require payments of this sort to be put through the payroll, so that NICs can be paid.

3 *Wages, salaries and fees*

O ur first job is to look at how income tax and NICs are paid on your ordinary pay, that is, the weekly, monthly or other payments you receive for your work. Extra payments, special payments and payments in kind are all dealt with in later chapters.

Let us begin by disentangling what you are earning from what is sent to your bank or handed over in your pay packet.

YOUR PAY SLIP

If your employer does anything other than hand you the cash you have earned (as with cash-in-hand payments for casual part-time bar staff), then you should receive a wages slip detailing what you have earned, what has been deducted, and what is left to be paid to you. This is required by law. The law also limits the rights of employers about the deductions they can make. The two laws that do this are the Employment Protection (Consolidation) Act 1978 and the Wages Act 1986. These are not part of tax or social security law, but do require full details of deductions for income tax and NICs to be set out. They also control the other kinds of deduction allowed against pay.

WHAT YOUR
PAY SLIP STATES

Full details of the laws about what can be deducted from your pay is beyond the scope of this book, but the example of a pay slip included on page 45 complies with all the legal obligations. These are that every payment of wages or salary should be accompanied by an itemised pay statement setting out the following details :

- **gross amount of pay**
- **amounts of all variable or fixed deductions and the reasons for them**
- **net amount of pay**
- **if different parts are to be paid in different ways, details of each part-payment.**

To keep things simple, the law allows the employer to give an employee a separate statement of any fixed deduction (for example, of union dues or a court order) to save having to repeat the information. However, any alteration to that order must be notified.

KEEPING RECORDS

Employers are also under separate obligations to keep detailed records of income tax deductions for the PAYE system, and of NIC payments for the modified PAYE system applying to NICs. Many employers keep all the necessary information for these on computer records, and repeat the information on the pay statement. The required records are :

- **date of payment**
- **amount of payment**
- **total pay to date (since start of tax year)**
- **total tax free payments to date**
- **total taxable pay to date**
- **total tax already paid**
- **total tax due to date**
- **amount of tax due with payment**

Equivalent details also have to be kept for NICs, except that these are not cumulative over the year but calculated separately with each payment, as we describe below. Separately, the employer must also keep details of each employee, including the employee's NI number and tax code.

A pay statement containing all the necessary information may look something like the example opposite.

WHAT YOUR PAY SLIP TELLS YOU

The example pay advice shows the treatment of a monthly paid individual making payments to a company pension scheme. There are no additions to basic pay, and the only other deductions are the required deductions under PAYE for income tax and NI contributions. The employee's PAYE code is 149L, a low code, and consequently the deduction for income tax is high. In many cases the code will be higher than this, for example 355L, and the tax lower. Is this the right PAYE Code? We looked at this in the first chapter. Remember, if the code is wrong, then the amount of tax deducted will also be wrong.

Wibble Workers

```
PAY ADVICE
Payment to        :     A Earner
Payroll number    :     0005744
Pay date          :     30.6.95
NI number         :     YH 33 44 33 44B
Tax Code          :     149L
```

Cumulative Tax Year Totals		Payments		Deductions	
This employment		Basic pay 1653.50		Superann	75.00
Gross pay	5050.50			Income tax	352.84
Superann paid	225.00			NI (D)	151.00
Taxable pay	4825.50				
Tax paid	1081.25				
NI to date	453.00				
		PAYMENTS 1653.50		DEDUCTIONS	578.84
		AMOUNT PAID £			1074.66

```
Payment made to Bank sort code 20-19-40 Account 76836204 by BACS
```

Note that the taxable pay is less than total pay. This is because the contributions of £75 a month to the company pension scheme are not subject to income tax, but are not included in the tax code either. We shall see in the chapter on pensions why contributions to some pension schemes are left out of this calculation. To ensure that no tax is paid on the pension contributions, they are treated as if they were tax-free pay. This only applies to private pensions. NI contributions to the state pension are not allowed as deductions for income tax purposes.

The NI contributions are being deducted at about

the main basic rate of deductions, but as the employee is in a company pension scheme, maybe the scheme is contracted out. If it is, then the employee should be paying a lower rate of contributions.

HOW MUCH PAY?

The pay slip shows gross earnings of £5050.50 for the year to date. How are income tax and NICs applied to this? What is "total" pay for these purposes? We saw in the first chapter that income tax is charged on something known as "emoluments" and NICs are levied on "earnings". We need to examine what is included in both to see on how much pay you will pay tax and NICs. Then we shall look at different kinds of cash payment, such as sick pay and holiday pay. Bonuses and similar special payments are dealt with in the next chapter, and payments in kind rather than cash in the chapters that follow.

Income tax liability depends on your total income (and allowable expenses) from your employment for the whole tax year, regardless of the weekly or monthly level of pay.

THE INCOME TAX YEAR

The PAYE scheme described in the previous chapter works on an annual basis. This is because the income tax is an annual tax, and the system restarts at the beginning of each tax year. Any rate changes, and changes in personal allowances, are made by the annual budget of the Chancellor of the Exchequer to take effect when the next income tax year begins.

For reasons of history rather than common sense the income tax year runs from 6 April in any one year to 5 April in the next. This is called a year of assessment or tax year, and is usually described as, for example, the tax year 1995/96. This means the tax year starting on 6 April 1995 finishes on 5 April 1996.

You pay tax in any tax year on all the pay you receive in that year less any expenses paid out in that year.

There may be some untidiness at the end of a tax year, but this is the general rule that applies. For example, if you are paid monthly, all your April earnings will be taxed when paid at the end of the month, even though you worked for some of the pay in the previous tax year. Whether you have earned the pay from the beginning of April in the previous tax year will depend on the precise terms of your job contract, but the way the PAYE scheme works gets rid of these technical differences.

If the PAYE scheme is working properly, you cannot pay tax unless you are yourself paid. You may sometimes receive pay without tax being deducted. This might happen if for some reason PAYE is not working properly. It may also happen with certain forms of benefits in kind or bonuses. In those cases, the tax office will need to collect the tax later. It can do this in two ways. First, it can alter your tax code for the next year, so as to collect the tax over that year in instalments. Alternatively, it can make a formal assessment, and demand payment direct. In most cases, if an assessment is made, then the tax assessed as due is payable in one lump sum on 1 January in the tax year, or 30 days after the date of the assessment, whichever is later.

Your total income tax bill takes into account all your income, not just that for your employment, and also your personal allowances.

You may have no other income than the pay from your job. But if you do have other income, your total tax bill will depend on all your income that year. This will be taxed at the income tax rates for the year, as set out in the previous chapter.

WHAT PAY IS TAXABLE FOR INCOME TAX?

Income tax is payable on all "emoluments", which includes all salaries, wages, fees, perquisites and profits of whatever kind received or receivable by you from your job. The rules for the lower paid are a little different (as we see below), but otherwise the rules applying to all other employees and office holders, and to all company directors are very clear.

You are liable to income tax on everything you receive because of your job, if it has a value that can be taxed. This applies whether or not the benefit is paid in cash, and whether or not it is paid under the terms of your employment contract.

There are specific exceptions to this rule for some kinds of income, and to take account of some kinds of deductions, but the starting point is that everything should be included. However, if you receive something which does not come from your job, it is not to be included. A genuine present from fellow employees because of a wedding is not taxable. Nor is a benefit which has no value for tax purposes, or one that is excluded by law from being taxed. What is regarded as coming from your job?

Anything that you receive by reason of your employment is taxable as part of your pay from the employment. Any payment of expenses or

any benefit which you, or any member of your household or family, receive from your employer is treated as being received by reason of your employment.

The only exception to this general assumption is where the benefit is received because of the personal or family relationships between the employer and employee. For example, if I employ my son to work for me, that does not turn my birthday presents to him into pay!

This rule makes it clear that you cannot avoid income tax by getting payments diverted to someone else. If my son or daughter receives a benefit from my employer, then I am taxed on it not them. However, if my son or daughter receives a benefit because he or she is also working for my employer, then the payment is taxed in their hands not mine.

Self-employed husbands (and wives) often employ their own wives (or husbands) so they can pay them and gain some tax advantages. This does not work if the husband (or wife) is an employee.

You may only deduct from your total pay those deductions and allowances expressly authorised by law.

Just because you think that you should be allowed a deduction for some expense does not mean it is allowable. The rules are very strict on this. That is what the chapter on work expenses covers.

IF YOU WORK,
YOU EARN

LOWER PAID STAFF

The rules are a little more relaxed on those regarded as lower paid staff. Who is "lower paid"? This does not apply to company directors (with the exception of a director employed full time in the company and who does not have a significant shareholding in the company, or of directors in non-profit or charitable companies, provided, in both cases, that their earnings are below the £8,500 limit). It applies to those employees whose total of earnings from a job is less than £8,500 a year (about £160 a week). The total of earnings includes all kinds of earnings, not just payments in cash. The rule is applied separately to each job of an employee. However, jobs cannot be split to exploit this rule. If the employments are with the same employer, they are regarded as one employment.

Part-time staff, particularly those working for only a limited time each week, or for only a limited part of the year, may find themselves in this rule, even though in total they are not "lower paid". For example, someone who is retired or who has another job from Mondays to Fridays and who gets a job on Saturdays only or for a fixed period of one month will be "lower-paid" for the Saturday job if it pays, say, £100 a day regardless of other earnings.

In the rest of this book, we describe those earning below £8,500 as lower paid if they fit within the rules described here, as a convenient short description.

INCOME TAX ON THE LOWER PAID

Lower paid employees are not caught by such strict rules as those that apply to most of us. Although there is little difference in the way that cash payments are taxed on the lower paid, benefits in kind and payments of expenses are treated in a much more relaxed way. As a general rule, payments of expenses can be ignored for tax purposes if they genuinely relate to work expenses. In addition, the value of benefits in kind for tax purposes may be lower - or zero - for the lower paid despite the taxable value being much higher on others. These differences are discussed further in the chapter on expenses and perks.

The outcome of these differences is that there are advantages for tax purposes in the lower paid being paid by benefits in kind (such as the provision of assets) even when there is no clear tax advantage for others.

LIABILITY FOR NI CONTRIBUTIONS

NICs are potentially payable by both employee and employer on all earnings from an employment each time those earnings are paid to the employee. The meaning of "earnings" is narrower than that of taxable employment income for income tax purposes. The system is also fundamentally different because the level of NICs is calculated separately for each earnings period, not on an annual basis.

You pay NI contributions by reference to the total earnings you receive from your employer in any one earnings period, regardless of your general level of earnings. So does your employer.

NICS EARNINGS
PERIODS

NICs are calculated by reference to the intervals at which any employee is paid her or his earnings from the employment. For example, if you are paid weekly, then a week is your earnings period, and your employer will be required to calculate the NICs due separately each week. The fact that you earn more in one week than the next is irrelevant. Similarly, if you are usually paid monthly, then your earnings period will be a month.

There are special rules to deal with unusual cases, such as those who receive payments irregularly. In these cases, the earnings period can be treated as being a whole year. This happens for all company directors. The year for NICs purposes is exactly the same as the income tax year, running from 6 April to 5 April.

There is some scope for reducing the total NICs liability of someone by playing around with payments periods. The Contributions Agency has powers to deal with avoidance of this kind, and will use them, for example, to demand that the payments be looked at over a year as a whole, if it feels that excessive avoidance is occurring.

You pay NICs on the total earnings you receive from your employer in each earnings period. So does your employer. You are not entitled to any deductions from those earnings.

No expenses are allowed to be set off against earnings for NICs purposes, even if they are allowed for income tax. Nor are there any personal allowances or other deductions for these purposes. You are liable to pay contributions on your total earnings without any deductions of any kind.

WHAT ARE EARNINGS?

Your earnings include everything you receive from your employment in cash or that can be converted into cash. You do not pay NICs on benefits in kind that cannot be changed into cash. Nor does your employer, except where you have a company car.

The different treatment of benefits in kind from cash payments is very important. This means, for example, that you do not pay NICs on the benefit of a company car. Your employer, however, has to pay a special contribution on the value of the car. No other benefit in kind is treated in this way. The NICs rules about cars are dealt with in the chapter on cars and mileage allowances.

The difference in rules between the lower paid and others for income tax does not apply for NICs purposes. In effect, the rules applying to the lower paid for income tax apply to everyone for NICs purposes.

Your liability to NICs will be calculated for each employment without regard to any other employment or any other source of income.

Again, this is fundamentally different to the income tax rule. Each job has to be treated separately. Income from self-employment is ignored, except that all earned income may be added to prevent the employee paying too much in terms of total NICs in a year. Income from any other source is totally ignored.

The rates at which NICs are paid by both employers and employees vary depending on the total earnings for the earnings period.

HOW MUCH NICS?

If your total earnings in an earnings period are less than the lower earnings level for the period, you pay no NICs. Nor does your employer.

The lower earnings level, which is adjusted annually to reflect changes in the value of money, is based on a set weekly figure. The

LOWER EARNINGS LEVEL

weekly level for 1995/96 is set out in the table. The annual equivalent of this figure is £3,016. However, remember that the contributions are not calculated on an annual basis except for company directors and some other special cases. Because of this, someone who receives little pay in one earnings period may pay no contributions at all, even though they earn a much larger sum in the next period.

LOW EARNINGS

If an individual regularly earns less than the lower earnings limit from a job, then no contributions will be paid at all. This will have the effect of saving both the employer and employee the cost of contributions. But if this is the only employment of the employee (or all employments are like this) it will also exclude the employee from any entitlement to statutory sick pay and statutory maternity pay (see below), and from any contributory benefits from the social security system such as unemployment benefit or the state contributory retirement pension.

For example, someone who works for a different employer on each day of the week, or who works for several people for a few hours each day (for example, a cleaner) may have earnings which total a significant amount, but may be below the lower earnings limit in respect of each employment. Often people working in this way are doing so through agencies. In that case, the agency is treated as the employer for all the employments, and the employee is therefore treated as having only one job.

If your earnings exceed the lower earnings limit in any earnings period, you pay NICs on all earnings up to the upper earnings limit for that period. Your employer pays NICs on all your

earnings without an upper limit.

Once your earnings are greater than the lower earnings level, then you pay a contribution on all your earnings, including those below the lower level. However, the rate applied to those lower level earnings is a much lower rate than the general rate of contribution.

As well as a lower earnings level, there is also an upper earnings level. This is roughly seven times the lower earnings level. The weekly level for 1995/96 is set out in the table. The figure is adjusted every year. The annual equivalent of the 1995/96 weekly figure is £22,880.

UPPER EARNINGS LEVEL

Employees' NICs rates and levels 1995/96

Lower earnings level : £58
Upper earnings level : £440

Standard rates of contribution :
Rate on earnings below lower earnings level: 2%
Rate on earnings between lower and upper earnings level : 10%

Contribution at lower earnings level (2% of £58) : £1.16
Contribution at upper earnings level (2% of £58 and 10% of the balance up to £440) : £39.36

Contracted-out rates of contribution :
Rate on earnings below lower earnings level   :   2%
Rate on earnings between lower and upper earnings level : 8.2%

Contribution at lower earnings level (2% of £ 58) : £1.16
Contribution at upper earnings level (2% of £58 and 8.2% of the balance up to £440) : £27.32

Where the total earnings of an employee exceed the upper level, the total contribution is capped. This applies no matter how high the employee's earnings go in that period. However, the employer pays contributions (at 10.2% in 1995/96) on total earnings.

AN EXAMPLE:

Ernie is paid £300 each week, and occasional bonuses. He is normally paid weekly. In October this year he is paid a bonus of £500. Ernie's earnings period is weekly, and no instructions have been given by the Contributions Agency to treat the bonus in any special way. Assume that the rates are those for 1995/96.

In a normal week, Ernie is paid £300. His NIC liability is 2% of the first £58, and 10% of the balance. He will pay a contribution of £25.36 on that.

In the week in which he receives the bonus, his total earnings are £800. He therefore earns more than the upper earnings limit, £440. He will pay a maximum contribution of £ 39.36 that week (see the table).

HOLIDAY PAY

In most cases holiday pay is treated in exactly the same way as ordinary pay for both income tax purposes and NIC purposes. The employer will deduct both when paying the employee. Any cash bonus added to the pay will be taxed as ordinary pay.

Employees have no independent right to holiday pay (or to holidays). This depends on the individual contract of employment. In some cases, employees have to fund their own holidays, and do so through annual savings from earnings. If pay is held back, to be paid later to the employee when the holiday occurs, then contributions and tax will only be collected when the payment is made.

In some industries, holiday pay is paid out of a central fund to which payments are made during the year. This makes no difference to income tax liability over the year as a whole. By contrast, payments made from the central fund are not subject to NICs.

Where an employee is given extra holiday, perhaps as a bonus, there is no effect on either income tax or NICs. It changes what the employee has to give the employer, not what the employer gives the employee.

SICK PAY

A member of staff who misses work due to sickness of any kind may be entitled to sick pay during the period away from work in one of four ways:

Statutory sick pay (SSP).
   SSP is payable by law by all employers to all employees who qualify for SSP under the statutory rules.

Incapacity benefit.
   This is payable on a contributory basis by the DSS. It is only payable where SSP is not payable, for example to those who fail to qualify for SSP but have paid contributions.

Contractual sick pay.
   Sick pay may be payable under the employment contract of the individual. There is no right in general law for an employee to receive anything other than SSP, but employment contracts often give more

generous rights to sick pay by agreement.

Personal income replacement insurance.
In these cases, the individual arranges a private insurance scheme to provide pay if the individual loses pay because of sickness.

STATUTORY SICK PAY

All employees are entitled to SSP if over 16 and under pensionable age provided that their employment contracts are due to last more than 3 months, that they have started work under those contracts, and that their normal weekly earnings from the employments are above the current lower earnings level. There are other limits to stop more than one social security benefit being paid at the same time.

INCAPACITY BENEFIT

In some cases where SSP is not payable (for example, where the employee has just started a new job), then he or she may claim incapacity benefit from the DSS Benefits Agency, provided enough NI contributions have been paid in the previous year. The Agency produces detailed rules for claims in these cases. A claim is made simply by handing the doctor's certificate stating that you are advised not to work over to the Agency with all details filled in (see the back of the form).

SSP is not payable for the first 3 days of any period of sickness. It is not payable for more than 28 weeks at any one time. Once the 28 week period is completed, the state takes over responsibility for paying benefit to the individual, who is normally then paid long-term incapacity benefit.

Where the individual is entitled to contractual

sick pay of at least the same level as SSP, then the contractual payment will dispense with the need to pay SSP. Sick pay is not payable twice.

SSP is treated as ordinary pay for most purposes. In particular, SSP is subject to income tax and NI contributions in the same way as ordinary pay. This, of course, reduces the value of the SSP when income tax is taken into account over the year as a whole. However, the weekly rate of SSP is below the lower earnings level of NICs, so if no other earnings are payable to the employee, then no contributions will be paid.

Entitlement to any contractual sick pay is purely for agreement between employer and employee. Any contractual sick pay will be treated in the same way as ordinary pay. It is subject, without any deduction, to both income tax and NI contributions.

CONTRACTUAL SICK PAY

Some individuals arrange sick pay, or additional sick pay, through private insurance policies. Premiums are paid when the individual is well, but if he or she should fall seriously ill, then a sum is paid (perhaps weekly) to the individual while ordinary earnings are not being received.

PERSONAL INCOME REPLACEMENT INSURANCE

Individuals are not entitled to a tax deduction for the cost of the premiums for this kind of insurance. At the same time, they are not taxed, nor made liable to NICs, on the benefits received from these policies, at least provided that the benefits are not paid out weekly for more than a year. If that limit is exceeded, although there would be no NICs liability, there might be a claim for income tax on the basis that this is unearned income.

4   Bonuses, prizes and special payments

Receiving an extra £1,000 from your employer is very pleasant. It is not so pleasant to discover several months later - and when you have spent it all - that the tax authorities want their share of it. You thought that it was a gift. They think it is part of your income, and should therefore be subject to tax. Who is right? That is what this chapter is about.

We will look at various kinds of bonuses, prizes and gifts, and when these can be free of tax. We also look at profit-related payments which can be free of some tax. Finally, we look at special payments, for example a payment to change the terms on which you work, or to encourage you to take up a job. As in other chapters, we check on the liability to NI contributions at the same time.

BONUS PAYMENTS

CASH BONUSES

The basic rule is :

If you get a cash payment, and it comes because of the job, it is taxable and subject to NICs.

But not every cash payment comes because of the job. For example, a present to someone getting married, a prize in a Christmas competition, a ticket which turns out to be a winner in the National Lottery, or a special tip on your birthday from a good customer are really prizes or presents, but a bonus at the end of the year because the firm has done particularly well is probably just an extra part of your pay.

Who pays for your bonus or prize? Is it paid by the employer, or is it from someone else? If the employer makes a payment to you, then the law normally assumes that that payment comes because of your employment. If it comes from someone else, it may still be treated as pay, but this will depend more closely on why it is being paid. For example, tips received from customers during ordinary working hours by taxi drivers or waiters are part of their income and are therefore taxable. A special tip "just for you and the family for the holiday" from a good customer at Christmas is a personal present.

Strict rules apply to extra payments, for income tax purposes, to all those who earn at least £8,500 from their job in any year (including all benefits). We explained this in the previous chapter. It means that those earning less that £8,500 in total have a slightly easier time. But we must first look at the rules that apply to most of us. There is no difference in the operation of the NI contribution rules for higher and lower paid staff.

HIGHER AND LOWER PAID STAFF

Are you entitled to receive the payment because of your job? A bonus, perhaps related to profits,

PAYMENTS FROM THE JOB

or your personal sales figures, or for completion of a job in a set time, paid by the employer and to which you are entitled under your terms of employment is always a payment because of your job. You can get some tax relief if the payment is *profit-related pay* (see below), but only if the conditions of that relief are met.

If the bonus is paid for extra work, it is still taxable. It would only fall outside the tax net if the payment was made for something not connected with your duties to your employer. For example, Gil gets a special bonus for work done out of hours in running a football team for children of the staff at his place of work. This is a voluntary task he has chosen to carry out, simply because he likes football and children. The directors of his business are also keen on football and are delighted at the success of the team. They therefore agreed to give Gil a special bonus. He was not working for them, and it was not part of his job. Nor was he entitled to or expecting the payment. The payment - sometimes called an "honorarium" - is not related to Gil's work, and is not subject to tax or NI contributions.

In such cases, the bonus should be paid separately from ordinary pay, and should not be subject to deduction of tax or NI contributions along with the pay.

CHRISTMAS BONUSES

A bonus to which you are entitled because of your job will be part of your pay. Even if you are not entitled to the bonus, but you expect to get the payment without any special duties or work, it will usually still be regarded as part of your pay. For example, if your employer pays you and everyone else a Christmas bonus, and does so regularly, then the amount of the bonus will be taxable. This is so even though the employer calls it a "gift". It is because the payment is made to you because of the job and not as a personal payment.

If, however, you do not expect the payment, or it is paid to you but not to all other staff, as a genuine personal Christmas present, then it will not be taxable. It has to be something personal rather than paid from employer to employee.

LONG SERVICE AWARDS

Sometimes a gift paid in cash is taxable, but a gift in the form of an article or item is not. For example, a cash bonus paid for long service at work is taxable. But a gift of, say, a watch or clock, for long service will not be taxed, provided that you have worked for the employer for at least 20 years, and the sum spent on the gift is not more than £20 for each year worked. The general rules for receipts not in cash form (usually called benefits in kind) are dealt with in another chapter. It is clearly better not to receive a long service award in the form of cash.

TIPS

Tips are payments made from customers that are, or are supposed to be, paid direct to the employee. For example, tips are customary to hotel and travel staff such as porters, to hairdressers, to taxi drivers and several other groups of employees. In some cases, the employer pays the person less because of the likelihood of tips.

SERVICE CHARGES

Tips are not the same as service charges, even if the employer makes clear that the service charge is handed on to the staff. Payments made for service charges are normally taxable in the same way as ordinary pay. They are also subject to NI contribution liability. This is because as between the employer and the customer, the service charge is a matter of contract, so it is really part of the price paid. A tip, even a recommended tip, is not.

WHO COLLECTS
THE TIPS?

Tips collected by employers and handed to staff are taxable in the same way as service charges. By law, they are regarded as payments arising from the job if they are usual or tips that staff expect. They are also subject to NI contribution liability. This means the employer must pay an NI contribution, as well as the employee, so the employer may wish to take that into account in sharing out the sums received.

Where staff look after the sharing of tips themselves, the rules are different for NI liability. Sometimes all tips are collected by a member of staff operating what is often known as a tronc. If the employer is not involved, then no NI contribution liability arises because the employer is not making the payments, so cannot add the tips to the payroll. This means a saving both to the employer and the staff.

Tips paid through the employer can be made subject to PAYE, so that income tax is paid when the tips are paid. Tips paid separately cannot be taxed in this way. But the Revenue has the power to impose an assessment on an employee receiving tips, and then demand the tax in a later tax year by altering the employee's tax code the following year. If the employee does not know how much has been received in tips, then the Revenue can impose their own estimate. Even if the employee thinks that is high, in practice it would be hard to challenge in the absence of evidence about actual amounts received.

PRIZES AND SUGGESTION SCHEMES

A cash prize or bonus for personal achievement at work from the employer is still part of the earnings from the job, even if there is no entitlement to it. This will apply to all kinds of cash bonus paid either related to your own efforts, or those of your team, or the entire staff. But this means that you get the award, only to see part of it taken away again.

Awards for doing your job well can be taxable even if they come from someone else. For example, manufacturers offer bonuses to staff in retail stores who sell more than set targets of their goods. These will also be taxable. Nor can the tax be avoided by making the prize a voucher rather than cash, or turning it into a benefit in kind.

To avoid prizes in these kinds of scheme being reduced by tax, employers can reach agreement that they will sort out the tax, at their own cost, with the Revenue. The prize then might appear tax-free to you, but it isn't. What has happened is that the employer has agreed that it will pay your tax for you. For this purpose, the employer must treat you as winning an award of enough to pay the tax due before paying the prize or bonus to you. Employers that wish to adopt these schemes are free to contact the Inland Revenue, which has a special unit dealing with the schemes.

TAXED AWARD SCHEMES

What a taxed award scheme amounts to is a scheme where you get a prize taken from a larger payment that includes the tax. For example, you have won a bonus under the monthly incentive scheme worth £75. The employer will report this to the tax authorities as an award of £100, from which tax of £25 has been deducted.

Nor is a taxed award free of NI contribution. In fact, this is even more complicated. If the award is paid in cash, then the employer must account for NI contributions as well as tax. To give you £75 may in this case cost the employer as much as £125. If the awards are not in cash form, then the NI contributions on the award are avoided - but not on the tax paid! So going back to the award worth £75, the employer must account for NICs both for the employer and the award winner on the £25 tax paid. Further, the NICs will count towards your eventual benefit entitlements to state pensions.

SUGGESTION SCHEMES

Suggestion scheme prizes are not caught by the rule that awards must be taxed. They can be free of tax if they are from a scheme which follows the approved form. For approval, the prizes must be given for suggestions made by staff outside the usual course of their duties. The prizes must be awarded once a cost-saving suggestion has been adopted, or be small gifts to encourage staff to make further suggestions. If it is your job to make proposals and suggestions, then any award for it is taxable. However, if you could not be reasonably expected to come up with those kinds of ideas as part of your job, the awards may qualify.

For example, an employer asks all staff for suggestions to help the competitive position of the firm generally. This may be done by putting a post box in the staff canteen for the suggestions. (One reason for collecting suggestions this way is that if the employer holds meetings for staff to discuss suggestions, then it becomes part of the job, so any award is taxable!) The suggestion from one junior staff member results in significant savings of cost in a key part of the employer's business. The employer can make a tax-free award of up to 10 per cent of the money saved over the first 5 years (or 50 per cent in the first year). For good ideas this can be a considerable amount. The employer can also pay out small "encouragement awards", of up to £25, to people whose ideas are good but are not used.

Finally, the schemes must be genuine. There must be no entitlements to receive awards under a scheme, and it must be at the discretion of the employer whether any payment is made and, if so, how much is awarded.

ROYALTIES

Where an employer uses an employee's idea that amounts to a new invention, artistic work or creation, there is an important legal question about the ownership of the property in the new proposal. Nobody has any rights to claim property in an idea, but every invention, image, or piece of written work, music or artistic creation belongs to its creator (or anyone to whom the creator sells it or gives it). This is what is usually known as intellectual property. Property of these kinds usually needs protecting in appropriate ways, for example by the registration of a patent, the claim of copyright, or the registration of a trade mark.

In most cases where a member of staff is employed in research and development by an employer, any new inventions or ideas will belong to the employer, and it will be the employer's right to register and exploit the property. But in some cases the rights belong to

INTELLECTUAL
PROPERTY

the employee. In these cases, the employee might be entitled to claim the property in the creation or invention.

If the employer pays for intellectual property rights, the money is paid not for the job, but for the use of the employee's invention. Payments of these kinds (often called royalties) are subject to special tax rules. An employee who finds herself or himself with intellectual property rights should consider taking expert advice (for example from a lawyer or patent agent) to protect the property rights and to ensure proper payment for those rights by the employer or any other person.

IF THE EMPLOYER PAYS YOUR TAX

Employers may agree to pay their staff "tax-free". They normally do this only in special cases, such as the taxed award schemes. This practice is not common in the UK, but it is carried out sometimes for an employee who comes from overseas and the overseas country has lower tax rates than in the UK. The difference, sometimes called tax equalisation payments, are always taxable.

TAX-FREE?

Such deals are rare because an employer cannot legally make a payment of earnings that is genuinely free of tax. All that can be done is to agree that a member of staff will be paid a set amount without any tax deducted from that amount.

For example, Tim has agreed with his employer that he will receive his pay free of tax, and that he will be paid £200 a week. This is treated both for tax and NI contribution purposes as being the sum he is paid after paying the income tax and NICs payable on his total earnings. In other words, his £200 a week is treated as being the sum payable to him after the usual deductions. So, for tax purposes, it will be the sum (perhaps £265 a week) necessary to allow PAYE to work before he is paid.

NI contributions are based on this gross sum, including the tax, so there will be NICs payable by both Tim and the employer at the right rate on the £250. If Tim is still to get £200, then the total sum must be increased further to take this into account (so Tim would be treated as earning perhaps £280 a week).

Alternatively, an employer may agree to pay an employee's tax bill. In this case, the payment of tax is itself taxable. So if the employer agrees to pay a staff member's tax bill on a bonus, then the tax bill is treated as being a further part of the bonus, and more tax is due (and so on, until the tax on tax on tax has either been paid, or someone has got fed up with the process!).

In other words, there is no such thing as a tax-free lunch! If you don't have to pay, then the employer does. The Revenue loses nothing.

PROFIT-RELATED PAY

Many large private-sector employers run profit-related pay (or PRP) schemes, but most schemes are run by smaller firms. In 1994, the number of individuals who were involved in a PRP scheme was approaching two million. They can be run by anyone other than government departments and public bodies (which do not make profits). The schemes are subject to complex rules and have to be approved and supervised by the Inland Revenue if they are to get tax advantages.

PRP SCHEMES

PRP schemes are not incentive schemes. Indeed, they are the opposite. They are a recognition of the profits previously made by the employer. The underlying idea is that employees should be prepared to expect their incomes to go up (and down) as the profits of their employers alter. If the business makes no profit, then a PRP scheme has nothing to pay out, and there is no PRP.

HOW PRP WORKS

Under a PRP scheme, part of the pay of all members of staff involved in the scheme is related to the employer's profits. The scheme will lay down how the profit is identified, and how much of the profits are available to employees. The scheme may cover the whole of the employer's activities, or only parts, but should include at least 80 per cent of the staff in the area of activities covered by the scheme.

Profit-related pay paid under an approved scheme is totally tax-free, but the amount of pay that can be put through a PRP scheme is subject to limits.

The first - and more important - limit is that the pay is genuinely profit related. This means that if there are no profits, there can be no PRP. There can be no guarantee therefore of the payment of PRP.

The second limit is a maximum of PRP that an individual can receive tax-free. The top limit for everyone is £4,000 a year. If the employee earns less than £20,000 in a year, including the PRP, the limit is lower, and is one-fifth of total pay.

PRP schemes do not have any effect on NIC liability. Payments of PRP are therefore subject to both employees' and employers' NI contributions.

PRP for Pip

Pip works for Squeak Ltd, which has a PRP to which Pip, and all other staff belong, except those who joined the firm in the last year. The audited profits of Squeak Ltd were very high last year. The PRP scheme registered for Squeak Ltd is based on a set percentage of the profits, so a large sum is available for distribution.

Pip earns £15,000 a year aside from the PRP. Pip can therefore receive up to £3,000 from the PRP free of tax for that year.

However, both Pip and Squeak Ltd must pay NI contributions on the £3,000 - probably at 10% in the case of Pip and a similar figure in the case of Squeak. Pip's bonus is therefore worth about £2,700 to him. Had Pip tried to earn that much extra in ordinary pay, the yearly pay would have to be increased by£4,100. But, of course, if Squeak Ltd made no profits, Pip's pay would only be the £15,000.

PAYMENT BY VOUCHERS

One way that payments can be made so that they are not cash payments, but have the same effect as cash payments, is payments by vouchers or similar documents. These have been used in the past to cut both income tax and NI contributions on payments, or to slow down income tax payments by avoiding PAYE deductions of tax.

In recent years, governments have changed the law to block off these ways round the tax laws. Vouchers and other ways of making payments in kind are dealt with in the next chapter. But there are also anti-avoidance rules dealing with what the law calls cash vouchers and credit tokens. In fact, these terms are misleading, because the provisions cover any form of voucher or document that can be exchanged for cash or can

VOUCHERS
AND TOKENS

entitle the holder to credit. For example, schemes under which the employee saves up stamps supplied by the employer to be turned into cash will be covered. So will the provision of a credit card or charge card for the employee to use to get cash.

The effect of any scheme like this is to trigger the anti-avoidance provisions. These require payment of income tax and NICs through the PAYE scheme on the value of the voucher. The value will be either the cash received by the employee, or the cost to the employer of providing the voucher. There are very few exceptions to this. These relate to such things as cheap travel for employees of companies such as British Airways or the rail companies.

PAYMENTS THAT CAN BE
TURNED INTO CASH

Another way round the liability to NICs, if not to income tax, has been that of making payments in a form which is not cash but could be turned into cash. For example, instead of me paying you a sum of money, I buy you gold, or diamonds, or unit trusts, savings certificates or government bonds, or any other investment or commodity that you can promptly resell on the market to gain the sum that you are due.

For income tax purposes, a payment in this way was treated as if it was a payment of the sum for which the items could be sold by the employee. There was an advantage until 1994 in that PAYE did not operate. Changes of the law that year mean that PAYE also applies to these forms of payment.

However, for NIC purposes, a payment in this

way was regarded as not being a payment of cash, and therefore not liable to NICs. This was not often used for staff generally, but for senior executives or those on special bonuses. The idea was to avoid having to pay the employer's 10% NI contribution on the bonuses, although the employees gained nothing. An employee would be owner, briefly, of some valuable wine or diamonds. These were then sold and the employee given the price (less any commission payments). This amount was the bonus. Sometimes, indeed, employees were caught out because they forgot that PAYE had not been paid on the amount received. The later tax bill, for up to 40% of the amount paid, came as a nasty surprise.

Since 1994, the nasty surprises have ended as PAYE has applied. In addition, the avoidance of NICs has been blocked, so these schemes, which had no other advantage, have been stopped.

GOLDEN HELLOS AND GOODBYES

An employer anxious to add a particular individual to the staff, or to remove a particular individual from the staff, may offer inducement payments to her or him to get a decision to come or to go. These payments can be of large sums, and have come to be known by exotic titles : golden hellos for payments inducing someone to come to a business; golden handcuffs for payments to induce them to stay; and golden handshakes when the employer is trying to get rid of someone. If the sums are not only large but also tax-free, then they can truly be called golden, but can this be done?

GOLDEN HELLOS

A payment made to induce you to join a new employer is normally regarded as an advance payment by the employer in connection with your future services for the employer. It is therefore liable both to income tax and to NICs in the same way as ordinary pay.

There are only two ways in which an inducement payment of this sort can be made non-taxable. Either it can be shown to be a genuine personal gift by the employer to the new employee (unlikely!), or it can be shown that the sum paid by the employer is paid not for future services but for some other asset, or for the individual to give something up in advance of the new job. In either case, the tax authorities could still argue that there is an element of advance pay in the arrangement unless it is clear that the newcomer is being paid fully for the job at the market rate.

For example, Newt is badly wanted by Pond plc as its new finance director. Newt is currently engaged in private practice in a lucrative post. Pond is prepared to make a generous payment to Newt to encourage the move. Pond could offer Newt a payment for giving up the present private practice - and perhaps giving up other advantages presently enjoyed. If so, Pond would have to make an unconditional offer of the payment to Newt, properly documented, and which did not affect the pay offered by Pond to Newt for the job. Just to offer an extra payment "when you sign" will not avoid tax or NICs.

GOLDEN HANDCUFFS

Employers sometimes think it is worth paying sums of money or other forms of incentive payment to staff to stop them leaving. For example, if an employee's present employer becomes aware that someone is trying to headhunt the employee from the firm, a special deal may be struck to get the employee to stay.

More generally, businesses like to keep their senior staff out of the hands of competition, and are prepared to make arrangements to encourage this to happen. Other payments are made when employers want their employees to accept different terms of employment, for example, different hours or wider duties.

All these payments will be regarded as arising because of the job, and they are therefore subject to both tax and NICs. For this reason, the most effective forms of payments to induce employees to stay are by means of incentive payments with a requirement that the individual loses if he or she leaves the job, and, for older staff, an attractive pension scheme.

Payments made when an employee leaves their job are usually a mixture of payments resulting from the job contract, and separate payments designed to make the employee leave immediately or to persuade the employee to give up the job contract and relinquish any rights to sue the employer or take action before the Industrial Tribunals.

GOLDEN HANDSHAKES

How much of the payment is taxed, and how much is tax-free, depends on the precise reason for the payments. This is also true of liability for NICs. Payments connected with retirement are dealt with in the chapter on retirement.

FINAL PAYMENTS FROM THE EMPLOYMENT

When an employee leaves his or her post at the request or demand of the employer, the employee will be entitled to payments of outstanding pay or other entitlements. For example, all employees, except those employed totally on a casual basis, will be entitled to a period of notice, and for payment for that period. Alternatively, the employee may have a fixed term contract, so that the employer is obliged to make a payment to compensate for the loss of entitlement for the rest of the period of the contract. The employee may also have foregone holiday entitlement, and be entitled to pay in lieu of this.

Where an employer requires the employee to leave the post immediately, then the employee will be entitled to payment for the full period of notice, as well as any additional payments that have accrued.

NOTICE PAYMENTS

Any payments in lieu of notice or of remuneration, or accrued holiday pay or similar entitlements paid to the employee because of contractual entitlements are part of the ordinary pay of the employee (even if the job has ended when they are received). They are therefore to be taxed and made liable to NICs accordingly.

REDUNDANCY PAYMENTS

If the employer is dismissing the employee by reason of redundancy, the employee is entitled to a statutory redundancy payment if he or she has worked for the employer for at least two years. These payments relate to the number of weeks worked by the employee for the employer and are a basic entitlement rather than a generous one. For this reason, employers will often pay more than the minimum if the employee agrees to "go quietly" and waive any rights against the employer in exchange for the payment. These payments do not arise from the employment contract. They are either compensation payments or gifts, but in either case they are not taxable in principle.

A golden handshake may be for a redundancy, but it may also be designed to persuade the employee to leave when the employer's request or instruction to the employee to leave is in breach of the employment contract. Here, any sum paid may be a compensation payment or ex gratia payment. Equally here, the principle is that these payments are not part of the employment.

To stop excessive abuse of these provisions, strict limits now operate on what is, and what is not, taxable. Under current income tax rules, the first £30,000 of any redundancy payment, golden handshake or other sum paid because of, or following, or connected with, the employee leaving the employment, is free of income tax. The rest is taxable. There are some special rules where an employment has involved time overseas when pay was not fully taxable in the UK. Individual advice may be needed in this kind of case.

For NICs purposes, the liability to NI contributions applies to all payments under the employment contract, or which the employee expects because of the job coming to an end. NICs are not due on any compensation for loss of employment or for any redundancy payment.

Where the reason for the payment is death or injury or disability, then any compensation payments or payments made in connection with the job ending under these circumstances are free of tax and NICs. Some of the payments made after the death or injury may be payments from the pension fund or insurance of the

PAYMENTS ON DEATH OR INJURY

employee, rather than from the employer. The position under pension funds is discussed later, but normally such payments are not part of the employment so cannot be taxed as such.

GETTING IT RIGHT

The position both on receiving a sum when taking up a post and receiving a sum when leaving at the employer's demand or request is complicated. The rules for NICs and income tax are not the same. There are parts of any sum paid which may be liable to tax and parts which may not be. Sometimes the exact amount will depend on the precise terms of the agreement. In addition, what may suit the employee best, for example in ensuring maximum use of the £30,000, may not suit the employer. It may therefore pay to get advice on this aspect of the payment from independent advisers or unions or professional associations before agreeing to the precise terms. Further, even where there are entitlements to receive payments free of tax, it is often for the employee to claim those entitlements, and it pays to do this promptly.

5   *Company share schemes*

*A*ll companies belong to their shareholders. They range from the smallest limited companies owned by a single person to the mighty multinationals whose shares are owned directly or indirectly by millions of shareholders. Sometimes the shareholders are spread across many countries. Companies exist (or are supposed to exist) for the benefit of their owners: the shareholders. What, therefore, could be more natural than schemes encouraging employees to become shareholders and therefore owners in their companies?

HOLDING SHARES IN LARGER COMPANIES

In practice, many people hold company shares as investments. These are the shareholders who intend to take no part in the running of the company. That is left to the professionals on the company's board of directors. What these investors want to see is the biggest return on their investments that can be obtained. This can come through dividends paid by the company to its shareholders, but it may also come through an increase in the market value of the shares. Anything an employee - particularly a key employee - does to increase the share value will therefore be advantageous to the investor. Again, what better than a scheme designed to encourage employees to maximise the value of shares by participating in that process?

While these aims have been encouraged by governments of various political colours, the total number of private individuals owning shares in this country has been decreasing. This is despite the fact that it is easy for someone with cash to invest in the shares of any company listed on the Stock Exchange. It is therefore open to employees of any large listed company to buy shares in their employer. Few do, except indirectly. In part this is because people have been buying shares indirectly in huge numbers in recent years. These are the shares bought and held by pension funds, investment trusts and unit trusts.

SAVINGS AND PENSIONS?

It is not always a good idea for an employee to invest her or his savings in the employer. Nor is it wise to encourage employees' pension funds to invest in their employer too heavily. If anything goes seriously wrong with the company they would lose not only their jobs, but also their pensions or savings. This was illustrated only too clearly by the plight of Mirror Group pensioners. Some had lost heavily when the removal of shares from their pension funds for use by Robert Maxwell's final dealings became known. Because of this, share schemes have been confined mainly to additional forms of pay to directors and employees, and they are not expected to replace pension provisions.

THE PUBLIC SECTOR

Share schemes cannot apply to public sector employers. This is because government departments, local councils and other government bodies are not companies, and cannot be bought. However, when government privatises companies it often gives benefits to employees of the new companies. Increasingly also, bodies such as universities set up private companies to handle part of their activities. They can provide shares or options to their staff. These benefits do come within the scope of this chapter.

TAXING SHARE BENEFITS

An employee receiving share benefits from the employer is taxable on those benefits, unless special rules apply. The employee, and employer, may also be liable for NICs on the benefits. VAT is not charged on share transactions. Stamp duty is payable on share transfers taking place through a sale, levied at 1/2% of the value of the shares sold.

For example, Exel plc decides to give each of its employees 100 shares at the end of the year. The shares have a nominal value of £1, but on the day of transfer their price on the stock market is £4.50. If the company makes a straight transfer of the shares to employees, they are free to sell them on the stock market when they receive them.

If this is how things are arranged, each employee will be liable to tax on the value of the shares they receive. This value will be based on the stock market value of the shares at the date they are transferred to the employee (here £4.50 a share), and not the nominal value. The employee will have to pay tax on £4.50 even if they do not sell the shares. NICs will also be payable on this amount by the employer and, often, also the employee.

If the employee pays the tax but decides to keep the shares, there may be further tax to pay. Companies pay a share of their profits to their owners, the shareholders, by means of dividends each year. Any dividends received will be taxable. The tax is actually paid by a credit at the time the dividend is paid, so most employees do not need to pay any further tax. If the shares go up in value, and the employee sells at a higher price than the market price when the shares were received, there may be capital gains tax (CGT) to pay. CGT is payable on the difference between the sale price and the price at which the shares are received. Deductions can be made for the cost of sales, and for the effects of inflation between the time of acquisition and the time of sale.

TAX ON DIVIDENDS

For example, E keeps the shares in Exel for 5 years, when they are worth £8.70. The cost of selling the shares is 25p each and inflation between receiving the shares and selling them is 20%. E received the shares at 450p and inflation of 20% increases that to 540p. The shares are sold for 870p less 25p commission, a total of 845p. The capital gain is therefore 845p less 540p, or 305p. E will be potentially liable to CGT on this amount at the same rate as income tax (25% or 40%) although no CGT may be payable since there is an annual exemption (£6000 in 1995/96). To encourage employees to get and to keep shares in their companies, schemes exist which avoid some or all of this tax.

Employers, with assistance from government, have created a range of different share schemes to help their employees gain a stake in their

TAX-APPROVED
SHARE SCHEMES

employers. The aim is to make them part owners of their own companies. If these schemes are used, the company and its employees can pay less tax than would otherwise be payable - also lower NICs.

Some schemes give shares direct to employees. They may do so unconditionally or with strings attached. Depending on the nature of the "strings", there may be tax advantages in these gifts. Sometimes, shares are put into trusts. Perhaps they come to belong to individual shareholders after a time, and perhaps they stay for the general benefit of employees.

Other schemes sell shares to employees at a discount. This may be linked with encouragement to save to buy the shares. These schemes may include an option to buy shares at a fixed price, often a price below the current market value. Each of these schemes is examined below.

HOLDING SHARES IN SMALLER COMPANIES

The position of shareholders in smaller companies, particularly private companies, is completely different. It is a condition of a company being a private company that it cannot trade its shares through the stock markets in the usual way. The holder of a share in a private company is often unable to sell it on the market. It may have no market value. Often the owner may be under a duty to sell it to the other shareholders. In the smallest companies, there will only be one or two shareholders. Frequently these shareholders are also the company directors and employees - or their relatives are. In these cases, some share schemes may not work.

Instead the owners have a different choice. Do they take the money out of the company through the shares, or through pay for their offices as directors or their work as employees? The right choice here may also cut taxes. This is dealt with at the end of the chapter.

PROFIT-SHARING SCHEMES

A profit-sharing scheme can be set up by a company to give shares to its staff with the cost financed out of the company's profits.

Let us leave aside the technicalities. These may, and should, be left safely to the experts, monitored by the Revenue. The idea is that the company sets up a trust or scheme to which it pays funds. The trustees or scheme managers use the funds to buy shares. Those shares can then be transferred to employees either straight away or after a time period.

Some companies have been running schemes of this sort for many years. However, companies have found (not surprisingly) that while some employees hang on to their shares, others sell them immediately. For tax purposes, it made little difference whether they sold or held, as either way they were taxed on the value of the shares gained.

To encourage employees to hold on to their shares, rules were introduced to give tax relief where the profit-sharing takes place through an approved scheme. The Revenue publishes detailed guidance about schemes, and schemes that follow this guidance are entitled to official approval. Once approved, they can pay benefits

KEEPING THE SHARES

in the form of shares to their staff without either tax or NICs being deducted.

APPROVED PROFIT-SHARING SCHEMES

The main feature of an approved scheme is that the shares must be held for a minimum period of several years. Otherwise there is no advantage to be gained from the scheme. The shares are therefore bought by the trust or scheme and held within the scheme. They must be held for a minimum of two years, or no advantages arise at all. To get the full advantages of the scheme, the shares must be held in the trust for five years before being transferred to the employee.

It is up to a company to decide if it has such a scheme, and how much money it puts through it. Indeed, despite the name, the company does not have to have profits, or to relate its payments to the scheme to its profits. The only actual requirement is that the company provides some funding. In practice many larger companies now have these schemes.

WHO IS INCLUDED?

A scheme must involve all employees, although the scheme can insist on a qualifying period of service before an employee takes part. If the scheme does have a length of service requirement, it must not be more than five years service.

Do all employees receive the same number of shares? In some schemes they may. However, the Revenue allows the entitlements of individuals to be varied provided everyone is allowed in on similar terms. This may allow such things as total pay and length of service to be taken into account - if this is what the scheme arrangements approved by the Revenue say. Another way of varying the shares issued to employees is to match them to existing shares held by the employee. For example, to gain 10 shares from the scheme you must already own 10 other shares in the scheme, which you have had to buy. There is also a maximum amount that any one individual can receive under the scheme in any one year. It is £3,000 a year, or, if greater, 10% of pay, subject to an annual top limit of £8,000.

EXAMPLE : CHER'S SHARES

For example, Cher works for Top plc, which has an approved scheme. Top plc pays funds to a trust set up by its advisers, into which part of Tops profits are paid. From this, Cher is entitled to an annual allocation of shares of a value equal to 5 per cent of her earnings from Top plc. In one year, her earnings were 40,000, so 2,000 £1 shares were allocated.

This happens every year, and the trustees hold the shares for Cher. At the end of the fifth year from the time when the shares were assigned to the trust, the trustees sign the shares over to Cher. When assigned to her, they are worth considerably more than when they were first bought for the fund.

For example, the 2,000 shares allocated to Cher five years ago are now being assigned to her. They are now worth £3,000. What tax does Cher pay? None. There is no income tax payable when the shares are handed over to the trust. Neither income tax nor CGT is payable when the shares are transferred from the trust. Nor are there any NICs to pay. Cher will only have to pay tax on the shares in two cases. The first is that, while the shares are in trust, Cher is entitled to the dividends paid out because of the shareholdings. Although the shares are in the trust, it is provided that the dividend income from those shares should pass directly to the employees. They will therefore be entitled (subject to income tax) to this extra income.

Cher might also have to pay CGT if she sells the shares at a higher price than the price at which she received them when they went into the trust. Any increase in value while the shares are in the trust remains free of income tax but not CGT.

The company gains too. It can treat the costs of the scheme as expenses to be set off against its profits for tax purposes. This is so even though all the money is promptly put back into the company in the form of the purchase of shares.

BUYING SHARES WITH SAYE

SAYE is Save As You Earn. It is the name for a savings account that allows you to save by monthly instalments with tax-free interest. It can last for 5 or 7 years. There is no tax to pay on the interest or bonus paid during and at the end of the savings period. However, the money must stay in the account for this time. If any interest or capital is taken out, tax becomes payable.

WHO RUNS SAYE?

SAYE schemes are run by most building societies and banks. You can get details about these schemes from your local branches. One advantage is that the savings are kept completely away from the employer at this stage. At the end of the SAYE contract, the money belongs to the employee whatever the arrangements with the employer. However, the savings scheme must, since 1995, be linked to a share scheme.

In this way SAYE is used to encourage the employee to save for, say five years. At the same time, the employee is given a share option on shares in the company.

SHARE OPTIONS

A share option is the right to buy a share at some future time. An option will normally either set a price for the share, or state how the price is to be set. It will also give a date on which or by which the share is to be purchased.

Unlike shares in profit sharing schemes, shares covered by options do not belong to the holder of the option until the option is exercised (and the price paid). Until that time, the employee does not receive any dividends in the company.

An option linked to a SAYE scheme will be for purchase of shares in the employee's company 5 or 7 years ahead. This is to fit in with the SAYE contracts. It also allows the employee to buy the shares at a good price. Normally, the price will be no more than the market price when the option is taken out. In some cases it can be as much as 20% below the market price on the day of the option.

At the end of the five or seven years, the employee receives the total amount of savings and interest from the SAYE account. He or she will then check the value of the share options. Unless the share's market price at the end of the period is less than the market price at the start of the period, the employee will make a profit by exercising the right to buy the shares at the set price. It is up to the employee whether to sell or keep the shares bought in this way.

How much might this be worth? The maximum amount of an SAYE contract is for savings of £250 a month (or £3000 a year). Sam decides to save £100 a month in this way over the 5 year period - a total of £6,000. To this will be added - tax free - a bonus equal to a further nine months savings, or £900. He will therefore have £6,900 to spend on shares at the end of the contract.

HOW MUCH?

Sam therefore agrees to take out options on shares in the employer up to that value. Sam's employer has a scheme that provides employees with shares at a discount of 20%. On the day that Sam decides to take out the options, each share stands at £3.50 on the Stock Exchange. Sam can therefore buy each share for £2.80. Sam therefore takes up options to buy just under 2,500 shares (2,466 to be exact), so that the whole £6,900 can be spent on shares.

Five years later, Sam's company has done rather well. The shares have risen from £3.50 to £6.00 a share. Sam cashes in the SAYE contract, having paid all 60 instalments, and rushes out to buy the shares under the option. The option entitles Sam to buy all 2,466 shares for the original price of £2.80. Sam hands over the SAYE money and acquires shares in the employer worth a total of £14,796 - all for £100 a month.

Is there any tax to pay? Sam pays no tax on the interest under the SAYE scheme. Nor is any income tax paid for the reduction from market price in the option or the gain made on the exercise of the option. The bad news comes if Sam decides to sell the shares, rather than keep them. Sam would be liable for the capital gain in the difference between the £6.00 a share received for each share sold less the price paid (adjusted for inflation over the 5 years). The price paid is £2.80. If inflation was, say 20% in total over the period, then the price would be treated as £3.50, and the gain would be £2.50 a share (less selling expenses).

Even then, Sam can make use of the annual tax-free amount of gains every individual is entitled to make before paying CGT. In 1995/96 this is £6,000. If Sam sold the shares in two lots, one this year and one the next, and had no other gains, this would avoid CGT too.

WINNERS ALL

The beauty of a scheme such as this is that those prepared to save cannot lose. Either way, they get back the SAYE sum. If Sam's company had done badly - for example the shares were worth £2.10 each at the end of the 5 years - Sam simply refuses to exercise the option.

EXECUTIVE SHARE OPTIONS

These are the schemes that have been hitting newspaper headlines in recent years, as high paid executives get large bonuses from share options in their companies. This has happened because the tax rules were changed to allow special share option schemes for company executives in 1988. The schemes provide that the option must be held not less than 3 years (and not more than 10 years) before being exercised. Therefore the first schemes with longer periods than three years are only now being cashed in.

The share option is similar to that in the SAYE scheme, except here the company will normally only grant options to full-time directors or its most senior staff. They can receive options worth up to four times their total pay for PAYE purposes. The price for the option must be not less than 85% of the full market price of the shares on the day of issue of the option.

No income tax is payable on the grant or exercise of these options. However, CGT is payable on the total increase in price from the price paid to the price obtained on sale (after taking inflation and expenses into account). The tax authorities will often expect to see up to 40% of the gain paid in CGT when the shares are sold. The advantage to the company, and to the executive, is that the company provides the executive with an opportunity to gain a large number of shares in the company. Yet there is no tax to pay unless the executive sells the shares. Of course, the executives (and colleagues) have to ensure that the company makes profits, so that the share price rises.

WHAT TAX IS PAID?

TAX SAVING IN SMALLER COMPANIES

Share schemes and options can work for small companies as well as large companies. But they only make sense when the employee (or director) is not already the owner of the company. In the smallest companies, the employees will already probably hold all the shares. There will be no easy market for the shares. If shares are to be sold by someone under an option scheme, it will be to the same group of people - perhaps the same person! - that has to buy them. In other words, the gain will not be on the open market.

Saving tax on shareholdings in smaller companies is an entirely different matter. Here, the choices are between whether the owners/directors/employees (often all the same people) pay themselves salaries as employees, fees as directors or dividends on their shares as owners.

EARNINGS OR
DIVIDENDS

It makes very little difference for income tax purposes whether someone who is a director and employee pays themselves directors' fees rather than a salary and bonus. If the directors lend themselves money ahead of deciding a fee, it will also be caught for income tax. NICs is calculated for directors on an annual basis. This is to prevent NICs avoidance by bunching payments during the year. Ordinary earnings will be subject to NICs in the usual way.

If, instead of paying out a bonus, the company decides to keep the profits and pay them out as a dividend, there may be a tax saving. The income tax on a dividend is 20% at the basic rate, not the usual 25% paid on earnings and other forms of income. The higher rate of 40% is however the same. More important, there are no

NICs to pay on dividends. The company (and often the director) avoids the NI contributions to be paid had the same sums been paid as earnings.

But does the company have to pay tax separately? Yes, it does - at an effective rate of 6% or so if all the profits are paid out as dividends.

This is now getting somewhat complicated: a special rate of income tax on dividends; no NICs; but an extra tax - corporation tax - on the company profits though they are all paid out as dividends. Which is the best way of paying profits? I am afraid that usually needs the efforts of an accountant, or at least a calculator, as there is no immediately obvious answer. A final point: if you do not pay NICs you may lose some benefit. At one extreme, you could decide to pay no NICs that year. This is because you only receive a dividend. If so, you will not have a qualifying year for pension purposes. Further, your dividend income will not count towards your rights to buy an occupational pension or personal pension, so you will lose that valuable tax relief.

The best answer is often a compromise - part payment by earnings, and part by dividend - with one eye on the total of all the tax rates and the other on the pension position.

WHAT IS BEST?

6   Company cars and travel

*U*ntil recently the favourite perk for most employees - after a pension - was the company car. For a period, the ambitious sought two or even three cars. Some still do. But now the weekend newspapers tend to carry long homilies on why company cars are not so good an idea. Employers are finding that car fleets for employees are increasingly expensive. Why is that so? It is because the rules have changed for both income tax and NI contributions. The tax and NI cost of having a company car has, in some cases, more than trebled in the last few years.

THE POPULAR CHOICE?

Many people are now better off with cash to buy their own car. Even so, a recent survey showed that about three quarters of all company executives with annual pay of over £20,000 had the full use of a company car in 1994. Many of them had free car fuel as well.

Those who did not get a company car, for example those in the public sector, might instead get a loan to help buy their own car or generous mileage allowances. The rules have also changed on these arrangements recently, and that is also not always good news.

Finally, there are many serious travellers among the growing number of people sent overseas by their employers with schedules which make the plot of Jules Verne's *Around the World in 80 Days* look like a picnic outing. How are they treated in connection with expenses?

COMPANY CARS

The tax (and NIC) treatment of a company car depends on the terms on which the car is made available to the employee, as well as the use made by the employee of the car.

At one extreme is the outright gift of the car to the employee, who may then do with it what he or she wants. At the other extreme is the limited use by the employee of cars from the company car pool. Under some schemes, the employee has only limited use of the car and is expected to make considerable use of it for business purposes. Under other schemes, the business use of the car (such as a second car) is minimal. Sometimes the employee is expected to contribute towards the cost, and in other cases the employee forgoes or loses some pay in exchange for the car. Each of these approaches may produce a different tax result. So also may the provision of a van or truck rather than a car.

This does not usually happen. If you are given a car because of your job, you are taxable on the car. If the car is new, the amount on which you

THE GIFT OF A CAR

would be taxed is the full cost to your employer of providing the car (and any accessories in the car). This may of course be substantially less than the amount that you would have to pay to buy the car yourself. This is because if the employer either is in the car business or is a fleet buyer of cars, it may be entitled to a significant discount against list price. If the car is second-hand, then the value for tax purposes is its market value at the time of transfer. This will be chargeable to the person receiving the car for the year in which it is received.

NI contributions are not payable on gifts in kind. This means that there is some potential saving to both employer and employee. Unless it was shown that the aim of giving the car was the transfer of a sum of money in indirect form, this would be a benefit in kind and therefore free of contribution liability.

The gift of a car for any other reason will have no income tax effect. Nor is any capital gains tax payable on the transfer of a car whether by an individual or a company. But the employer may have to account for VAT on the gift as if it were a sale if making a gift of a car to an employee.

THE LOAN OF A CAR

This is the usual arrangement. The employer lets the employee have the car for personal use (including business use) on set terms. These may prevent anyone else driving the car, or may allow only named people to drive it. The employee would normally be prevented from hiring the car out or otherwise making money directly from it. And, of course, the employee is unable to sell or lease it to anyone else.

Because so many cars are offered as perks by

employers, there are special tax rules dealing in detail with them. The rules were felt necessary because the provision of a car could save the employee (and employer) considerable amounts of income tax. But they did not tax cars on their full values. Instead they were taxed on a "tariff" value which was significantly below the market value of the use of the car. Besides which, there were for a long time no NICs on these arrangements.

There were several reasons why cars were treated leniently by the tax laws. Some were political, and had to do with the love affair that people seemed to have with their cars. Perhaps also for a time it had something to do with the fact that the British government, via what was for a time British Leyland, was itself a car manufacturer and a major seller of company fleet cars. Now not only has the government stopped making cars, but the love affair seems to be coming to an end.

LETTING CARS
OFF LIGHTLY

Since 1994, someone supplied with a car by reason of their work will pay an annual income tax charge based on the price of the car, and they together with the employer will pay a special Class 1A NI contribution charge based also on the price of the car. How much tax and NICs will be paid depends on the use to which the car is put.

... AND NOT SO LIGHTLY

The new 1994 rules provide that the amount of tax paid by someone who has a car made available with the job depends on the list price of the car. This means the published

THE TAX VALUE OF A
COMPANY CAR

manufacturers' list prices for individual cars sold just before first registration. This is normally the inclusive price published by the manufacturer as the price of that model including all standard accessories (and the cost of fitting them) and delivery costs, together with any VAT or other taxes payable. The cost of any non-standard accessories will be added to this. The fact that the employer has bought a fleet of cars at a heavy discount is not relevant to the tax position. The value of the car for NI contribution purposes is the same as that for tax purposes.

There is no minimum figure for liability, but at the seriously expensive end of the market, there is a maximum price of £80,000.

CLASSIC CARS

There are also special rules for classic cars. These are cars over 15 years old with a market value of over £15,000. If, as will usually be the case, the market value is greater than the list price of the car when new, the tax and NI charges will be based on the market value.

THE NEW RULES

What is new about these rules? Before 1994, cars were valued at a tariff price that depended on the size of the car engine. Accessories were ignored. This meant that the notional value of many cars (especially classic cars and those just below the top of an engine size range) was considerably below the tax based on list price. It also caused major distortions to buying policy as cars were designed to fit in with the engine sizes. By contrast, in some cases the old tariff price was higher than the list price. These cases were however the exceptions.

For example, before 1994 the tax cost of a 2005 cc car was significantly more than a 1995 cc car, though both were usually called 2 litre cars. Now the price will depend purely on the list price of the two cars, which may make the 1995 cc car more expensive than the 2005 cc car.

If the car is provided to the employee with non-standard accessories added, the cost of these accessories may be added to the list price for tax purposes to find the full value of the car. The cost of all non-standard accessories added to the car at the time the employee first has it is to be counted. The only accessories excepted are mobile telephones and accessories added because they are necessary for the job. If, for example, the car is adapted to carry specific work-related items securely, that cost can be ignored. A CD-player cannot be.

PRICE INCLUDES
ACCESSORIES

If additional accessories are added later, then they may be the subject of an addition to the tax charge. All accessories totalling over £100 are to be added to the car's price unless they are direct replacements of accessories already fitted.

The price of an accessory is, again, to be the list price including fitting costs.

Mobile telephones are excluded from the general charge on accessories because they are subject to a separate tax charge (but not an NI charge). If an employee has a mobile telephone made available during the year which can be used for private calls, the employee is treated as having received a taxable benefit of £200. That is, the employee is treated as having, for tax purposes, earned £200 extra. At 25% income

MOBILE TELEPHONES

tax, this will cost the employee £50 extra tax.

The employee is subject to the charge if they have any private use of the phone, unless the full cost of private use has to be met directly by the employee. The fact that the private use is less than £200, or less than the tax actually paid, is irrelevant.

HOW MUCH TAX?

The employee will be treated in any tax year as earning a percentage of the list price (including accessories) of any car provided for non-business use.

Apart from the price, two factors are taken into account in working out the tax payable on the car :

The age of the car
If it is over 4 years old at the end of the tax year, a discount of 1/3rd applies to the price on which the tax is payable;

The amount of business use
There are three levels of use depending on the number of business miles driven during the year. A business mile means a mile driven on business rather than for private purposes. The tax charge varies between the levels :

Business miles	Percentage charge
Under 2,500	35
2,500 - 17,999	23 1/3
18,000 and over	11 2/3

This tariff applies to everyone other than the lower-paid. Someone earning under £8,500

will, however, not have to pay any tax on the
use of a car. Nor will NI contributions be paid.

EXAMPLE : KERMIT'S CAR

Kermit has been given a new frogmobile, which the employer bought (at
a heavy discount) for £8,000. The manufacturer's standard list price for
the car is £14,000. Because the employer secured the car so cheaply,
Kermit has been invited to nominate non-standard accessories for the
vehicle. Kermit has asked to have a new SupaBlasta sound system
installed in the car, and this is costing a further £2,000, a total cost to the
employer of £10,000.

Kermit expects to use the car for only a limited amount of business, as he
spends most of his time at the company headquarters. The main use of
the car, apart from leisure, will be travel to work.

For both income tax and NI purposes, the taxable value of the car is its
list price with accessories. This will be £16,000.
If Kermit is using the car for less than 2,500 miles a year, then both tax
and NICs are payable on 35% of the £16,000, or £5,600.

How much will this cost Kermit and the employer? Kermit has to pay
extra income tax on the £5,600 at either 25% or 40%. If Kermit is a
basic rate taxpayer, the income tax is £1,400 or about £116 a month.
The employer pays the special Class 1A NI contribution at 10.2% of the
tax value of the car, or a further £571 a year.

If Kermit were to make heavy business use of the frogmobile, the tax
charge will drop to a third of this figure when the business mileage
exceeds, on average, 1,500 miles a month. So will the NI charge. This
mileage excludes travel to work. The tax charge will also drop by 1/3 if
Kermit keeps the car for four years.

Kermit will not be liable to any VAT on this use of the car. Nor will
Kermit's employer.

NICS ON CARS

CLASS 1A NICS

The NI contributions charge on a car is separate from the income tax charge. It is also levied through a special Class 1A NI contribution that applies only to the employer. In effect, the employer that provides a car to an employee has to pay a 10.2% charge on the same tax value as that used for the employee. This charge does not apply to the employee even if the employee is earning less than the upper earnings limit for contributions.

Although the contribution is payable as a NIC, because the employee has to pay nothing, there is no entitlement to benefit based on the car contribution.

THE TOTAL TAX AND NICS BILL

The Kermit example shows the total value of the car charge for both income tax and NICs. For someone paying higher rate tax, the highest cost is 40% (the tax rate) of 35% (the percentage charge if there is little business use), of the price, with a further 10.2% of 35% paid by the employer.

For each £1,000 of the price of the car and accessories, this amounts to £140 income tax and £36 NI contributions a year.

A SECOND
COMPANY CAR?

If an employee is given the use of two (or more) company cars, each is taxed separately on its own value and business use. As few employees will be able to log up enough business miles on the second car to qualify for a tax reduction on the grounds of business use, second cars are usually subject to a tax charge at the highest level. This can mean that they are not a good idea, even if a single car is.

Apart from the obvious points of buying cars with lower list prices, adding fewer accessories, and using the cars for more business miles, the answer is broadly no, unless the employee pays directly for the car or its use.

CAN THE TAX COST
BE REDUCED?

The tax charge is reduced if a member of staff pays either a capital contribution towards their car, or pays towards the private use. If an employee pays a lump sum towards the cost of the car, the list price is reduced by that sum, up to a maximum of £5,000 contributed. But is it worth paying? You have to find the cash, and lose, say, building society interest on it while it is tied up in the car. You will presumably not get it back. So, £1,000 paid towards your car costs you rather more than £1,000 - especially if that £1,000 comes out of taxed income. But it will save you at most just over £420 in tax (at the 40% rate). That is not a good bargain.

Nor is it a good idea to pay towards the running costs of the car. If you pay, say £1,000 towards the year's running costs, the amount you pay is set off against the taxable value of the car. This reduces the price of the car for this year only by that amount, saving at most £400 in tax. That leaves you £600 out of pocket.

Contributions may be required by the employer for its own reasons. They do not usually cause tax savings or impose a tax charge.

CAR OR CASH?

Sometimes employers offer cash and cars as alternatives. In a sense, if the employee chooses a company car they are losing a set amount of salary. This looks like payment for the car. Strictly, depending on the wording of the employment contract, and any separate agreement for the provision of the car, the loss of salary may be independent of the car. If that is so, then the employee losing salary merely pays less tax on the salary but pays the car tax charge instead. The employee without a car pays tax (and where appropriate NI contributions) on the actual salary. Which is the better deal depends on the precise costs involved, as we note next.

ARE PERK CARS GOOD IDEAS?

That depends on you and the car, and how much you will use it both for business purposes and privately. The real comparison is with the cost of buying a car yourself and using it for the same business purposes. That needs to take into account any mileage allowances the employer will grant you.

You also need to consider how you will pay for the car. Will the employer lend you the money, or some of it? If not, where will you get it? If you have to borrow it, do not forget to count the cost of borrowing. If you have to raid your savings, you need to count the cost of the lost interest on the savings.

In addition, if the car is yours, you lose the depreciation (though, of course, you may buy a car that is not new). You will also have to pay repair or warranty costs, and suffer any inconvenience while the car is serviced or breaks down. Then you need to check who pays for the car licence, the insurance, and membership of a breakdown service.

Working all this out is not an easy sum. It will prove that cars are never cheap, but it may sometimes prove cheaper to have your own car than one from the firm.

One way out of both the cost and the tax charges is the use of pool cars. If the employer runs a pool of cars available generally to the staff, then individual staff members do not get charged on car use. But to be a "pool car", the car must not be assigned specifically to any one member of staff.

A pool car cannot be made exclusively available to any individual member of staff. Further, the pool car must be mainly used for business purposes. An employee cannot normally take it home overnight. While the tax authorities may ignore an employee taking the car home on a few occasions in order to get an early start, that does not mean every other day.

The pool car provision does allow a company to keep back-up cars for its staff without the staff concerned being taxed on the back-up car.

THE CAR FUEL CHARGE

Over half of those who are supplied with company cars by their employers are also supplied with free fuel. This means that they are given the fuel to run their cars at no cost to themselves. The petrol or diesel may be supplied directly by the employer, or through an account in the employer's name at a local garage. If the employer refunds the cost to the employee, this may be taxed on the cash provided subject to the rules discussed in the chapter on cash benefits.

The fuel charge on an individual is based on a tariff (the same tariff as used to apply to cars before 1994). This fixes the charge at a set sum of money dependent on the engine size of the car, and whether it uses petrol or diesel. It does not apply to lower-paid employees.

Fuel Charges

The tariff for 1995/96 is :

Engine size	Scale charge	
	petrol	diesel
0 - 1,400 cc	£670	£605
1,401 - 2,000	£850	£605
2,001 +	£1,260	£780

Cars without cylinder capacity are charged in the same way as cars of 2,001 cc capacity.

For example, Ida gets free petrol with her 1,500 cc company car. She gets the fuel from the local garage where she is authorised to take fuel that is charged to her employer's account. She is treated as having additional income of £850 a year for tax purposes. As she pays at the basic rate, this costs her £213 extra income tax a year. The employer also has to pay a Class 1A NI contribution on £850.

PAYING FOR FUEL

If the employee pays for private fuel, the scale charge is not imposed. If the employee only pays part of the cost of the fuel used (directly or indirectly) then there is no reduction to the scale charge. No tax is saved by the employee meeting anything less than the full private cost of fuel used.

OTHER PERKS

Besides buying the car, the employer will often bear the running costs of the car. These are regarded as taxed along with the value of the car by the tax charge, so do not give rise to any further charge. There are exceptions to this general rule for mobile telephones (already noted), car parking and chauffeurs, and for any benefits which are in reality separate from that of the car and fuel.

CAR PARKING

Free parking at the place of work is not a taxable benefit if provided by the employer. If the employer pays the employee to park near the workplace, then the amount that the employer pays the employee is taxable. The employee is not often going to be able to argue for a tax deduction on the basis that the parking charge is a necessary expense (see the chapter on work expenses).

It is therefore important to ensure that the employer, not the employee, pays for the parking at or near work.

COMPANY DRIVERS

The cost of a company driver, or chauffeur, driving a car being used by an employee for private purposes is taxable, even if the cost of the use of the car is not. The tax charge will be based on the actual cost of the driver's services, apportioned to take account of the extent of the private use by that employee.

USING YOUR OWN CAR

If, instead of having a company car, you use your own car for work purposes, how is this treated for tax purposes?

Many public sector staff are not entitled to a car from their employer (except on a pool basis), but instead get financial help from the employer towards travel costs and towards the cost of buying the car. We need to note how cash help of these kinds are taxed, and also what deductions, if any, are available for travel costs against the earnings from the employment.

MILEAGE ALLOWANCES

The usual form of help from an employer to employees using their own cars for work purposes is through a mileage allowance. The individual is reimbursed at a set rate for each mile actually driven on official duty. This of course excludes travel from home to work, and private jaunts.

The rate at which the employer pays back the employee can vary widely. Those working for government service can recover costs at a set rate that is adjusted each year. Other employers set their own rates, which may be either generous or mean. A generous rate will include an allowance for wear and tear, and may be designed to leave the employee with a small profit per mile. The average rate will reimburse only the direct costs such as petrol.

The tax authorities recognise that the cost of running a car is in reality far more than the "average rate" as we termed it. Each mile involves using a bit of the capital cost of the car, of its car licence and insurance, and its tyres and so forth, as well as petrol and oil. But the tax authorities also recognise that excessive car allowances can be used to hide extra income. The middle way between these extremes is a Revenue scheme known as the Fixed Profit Car Scheme.

The FPCS, for short, is a voluntary scheme, but is widely used. Under FPCS, the Revenue allow a set mileage allowance to be paid tax free to employees provided that the employees do not claim any further expenses for running their cars. The employers may also be released from the general obligation to make detailed returns of the mileage expenses paid to their employees.

THE FIXED PROFIT
CAR SCHEME

If the employer pays over the FPCS rates, then the extra amount is taxable in full. If the employer pays the FPCS rates or lower, no tax is collected. Because the payments are usually regarded as refunds of expenditure if at these rates, there will also be no NI contributions on the payments.

The scheme allows a high mileage rate for the first 4,000 miles of travel in a year. This is intended to contribute to the basic charges on the car such as insurance, the car licence and depreciation in the car's value. For mileage in excess of the first 4,000 a lower rate is paid, to meet only the running expenses (petrol, oil, servicing and so forth).

The scheme also takes into account the size of the car's engine in basic engine sizes of 1000 cc, 1500 cc, and 2000 ccs. An average rate midway across the range is also allowed for employers that run a flat-rate scheme.

In 1995/96 the FPCS rates were 38.5p for the first 4,000 miles at the average rate and 21p below that. This was half way between the rates for cars over 1000 cc and cars over 1500 cc (34p and 19p for the smaller cars and 43p and 23p for the larger cars).

CLAIMING EXPENSES

All employees have an alternative to the FPCS for income tax purposes. They can declare their mileage allowances and claim instead a deduction for the costs of the car directly. The costs include both the revenue costs and the capital costs, although these are allowed under separate tax rules.

The travel costs have to be shown to be necessary in the course of the employment under the rules explained in detail in the chapter on work expenses. That means that the travel is required of anyone doing that particular job. For more details see chapter 8.

CAPITAL COSTS

You can also claim a tax allowance against your earnings for the capital cost of buying a car used for work purposes. You can claim a capital allowance (these are also explained in the chapter on work expenses).

CAPITAL ALLOWANCES

This is best explained by an example. Roc buys a car for £5,000 second hand, paying cash for the car. It will be used by Roc for half its usage for business purposes and half for private purposes. Roc will keep a mileage record of the car's use to substantiate this if asked. Roc has, in effect, bought the car half for business purposes. Can capital allowances be claimed?

Roc can claim a capital allowance on the part of

the price incurred for business purposes. It does not have to be shown that the car was necessary for the employment, only that it is in fact provided partly for use in the performance of the employment.

If the car had been provided only for the business by the employer, the capital allowance would have been 25% of the cost of the car in the first year, and 25% of the unallowed cost in each subsequent year. An employee is entitled to the same allowance as the employer. Where the car is only part used for business purposes, the capital allowance is apportioned. In Roc's case, this means that the 25% allowances are given on half the £5,000, that is £2,500.

The tax value of the capital allowance will therefore be :

In year 1 : 25% of £2,500 or £625

In year 2 : 25% of £1,875 (£2,500 less £625) or £468

In year 3 : 25% of £1,407 (£1,875 less £468) or £353

and so on down. Roc can claim a deduction for the capital allowance against earnings of £625 in the first year, £468 in the second year and so on.

This example conveniently assumes that Roc bought the car right at the beginning of the year. In fact, it can be bought at any time during the year, but if it is, the capital allowance also has to be apportioned on a monthly basis. For example, if Roc bought the car three months into the year, only 9/12ths of the allowance will be granted in the first year. (This will increase the amount allowable in the second year, but that's a whole year later!)

COSTS OF BORROWING

The capital cost of the car includes the actual price paid for the car, but does not include any allowance for the costs of borrowing the money to buy the car, or the finance costs hidden in a hire-purchase arrangement. No tax relief is available for the interest payments under the capital allowance provisions. Instead, any claim has to be made under the separate rules for claiming a deduction for payments of interest. These rules allow a tax deduction for the interest incurred on buying a car on which capital allowances are claimed in the way just explained.

As with capital allowances, the interest payments will be apportioned if the car is used both for business mileage and private mileage. The interest is an allowable deduction for the first three years of the loan only. Strictly, the interest is disallowed if it falls due more than three years after the end of the tax year in which the loan is taken out. This is one explanation of the commercial arrangements to pay for cars over a three year period. It is also the length of time that many people hold new cars before selling them.

CAR LEASING
ARRANGEMENTS

An alternative way of getting a car is to lease it. Leasing involves, in effect, renting the car for a set period at a charge which allows both for the price of the car and for the finance costs of paying for it. The lease may end with a provision allowing the lessee to buy the car either at its then market value or possibly more cheaply. Leasing costs are all revenue costs and do not qualify for capital allowances. They will qualify for deduction if within the usual deduction rules.

Before 1995, leasing arrangements could prove costly because of the VAT. The lessee had to pay

VAT on the lease, and unlike a business was unable to claim it back. But the company leasing the car was unable to claim back the VAT on the car when it bought it. The result was a double VAT charge. The cost of the VAT on the car can now be recovered, removing this double charge, and making leases in these conditions more competitive.

This can be dealt with much more simply, although the rules are different for the lower paid, and foreign travel is treated in a more relaxed way than travel in this country.

OTHER TRAVEL COSTS

In principle, anything spent by or for an employee on travelling by rail or air is taxable, but the employee can claim a deduction for necessary costs. As long as the employee is travelling at work and not to work, and the travel is part of the job, this will present no problem. The travel will be necessary, and therefore its cost will be deductible. It is only if the travel has some other purpose (like a disguised holiday) that the Revenue could challenge it. Nor will there be NICs to pay on refunds or payments in connection with travel.

TRAVEL IN THE UK

In practice, for both income tax and NICs, the employer will usually reach an agreement with the Revenue (under the P11D procedure) that travel costs of these kinds, when certified as part of the job, will not be liable to tax. When that happens, the employer will not collect PAYE tax or NICs on the travel costs, and the employee is not expected to put the costs in their tax return.

FOREIGN TRAVEL
EXPENSES

Where an employee is required to carry out all or part of the job overseas, the allowance of travel costs is more relaxed.

Whether the travel costs are met direct by the employer, or by the employee, the employee can claim a deduction equal to the costs (ie can avoid tax) on the travel costs from anywhere in the UK to the overseas workplace, and at the end from the workplace back to anywhere in the UK. There is no limit on this (assuming the money is actually spent), provided that the travel is only for work reasons. If the travel is also for some other purpose (such as visiting relatives) then only part of the cost is allowable.

In addition, the employee is also entitled to relief on the cost of board and lodging outside the UK. This again applies whether the employer pays the costs or the employee pays them direct.

Further, if the employee is going to be overseas for more than 60 days, then the travel costs include costs for the employee's wife or husband, and also children under 18, to travel out with, or to, the employee. This is subject to the limit of two return trips a year. There are certain technical restrictions on these allowances and it may be worth checking up on how precisely these rules will apply before incurring major expenditure on them.

7 Perks and expens accounts

*I*t has been common for many years for employers to pay their employees at least in part in non-money form. Indeed, in the past the famous Truck Acts were needed to prevent some employers paying their employees in such a way that they were only able to spend their earnings in the company store. Nowadays it is the employer and employee who sometimes work together to find methods of payment that do not have money value, in order to reduce the impact of income tax and NI contributions on the form of payment.

There have been two methods in particular that were widely used in past years to provide benefits to employees without the full rigours of tax applying: the expense account, and the rules aimed at non-cash perks. Both are now subject to rules which catch them for tax purposes at least to some extent. But there are still some advantages left.

EXPENSE ACCOUNTS

An expense account can exist in two forms. First, the employer can let the employee incur expenditure up to a preset limit over a stated period without further authorisation. Normally, the employer will require evidence from the employee about the individual items of expenditure. Alternatively, particularly with senior staff, the employer may give the employee open authority to incur expenditure in connection with the job, perhaps by giving the employee a company credit card or the authority to incur bills with specific suppliers.

It is for the employer to consider how to ensure the correct operation of such accounts. As between employer and employee penalties for abuse can be severe, ending in instant dismissal and criminal prosecution. But the tax authorities were forced to recognise that not everyone kept such a close watch on the way expense accounts were used, and it was felt that they were widely abused by those seeking to meet personal expenditure without paying tax.

A CATCH-ALL RULE

To stop this form of abuse, a general rule now applies to all but lower-paid employees. It is that all sums made available to an employee through an expense account or similar arrangement are to be treated as part of the taxable pay of the individual. It is then for the individual to show that the expense is truly work expenditure by means of a claim for a matching deduction for work expenses.

As we see in chapter 8, it is not easy successfully to claim a deduction for tax for work expenses. This is therefore a rigid rule.

Treatment of expense accounts for NIC liability can be even stricter. This is because no

NICS

deduction for expenses is available for NICs purposes. Yet, where an employer meets the cost of an expense direct with someone providing something for the employee, there will be no liability to NICs. The result here can be uneven, and sometimes unfair. With this in mind, the government announced in the 1994 Budget that it is changing its approach to expense accounts for NICs purposes.

In future, if an employer complies with the P11D procedure explained below, the employer (and employee) will get clearance for NICs purposes, as well as the tax clearance in most cases. At the time of writing, full details were still awaited of the procedure to be used to achieve this.

LOWER PAID

The strict income tax rule does not apply to lower-paid employees, to whom no special expense account rules apply. For them, the general rules still operate. These state that the refund by the employer of genuine work expenditure by an employee is not part of the employee's pay. No tax return is needed and there are no tax consequences. Of course, if the refund of money is for a non-work expenditure, that is part of the employee's pay.

P11D PROCEDURE

Precise application of the expense account rule would impose a burden on many employees, as well as their employers and the tax authorities, to examine individually many claims for the refund of perfectly legitimate expenditure.

To avoid too much administrative complexity, the Revenue have adopted some short cuts, which are often operated to the benefit of employees without them being aware of the problem. The main one is a form called P11D which employers have to return to the Revenue setting out in detail the expenses paid out to employees and why they are paid out.

First, an employer must reach agreement with the local tax inspector that expenses (or some kinds of expenses) paid to employees would be liable to tax but at the same time allowable as expenses. The rules for such allowances are set out in chapter 8, so we will not repeat them here.

Agreements may be reached for all kinds of expenses paid to or for employees, or set kinds. For example, the agreement may cover travel costs, or the refund of specific employment costs met by the employee and refunded to them.

Once an agreement is in place, the employer reports details to the inspector on form P11D. If the tax inspector accepts the return, it is usually accepted that the expenses paid out are accepted. If that happens, no further tax is due from the employee.

It is for this reason that employees are not often asked for details of expenses paid to them. Nonetheless, the underlying tax position is not affected by this procedure. Expense accounts are not a way of cutting taxes. If they are used to meet unauthorised bills which are not work expenses without the employer knowing, then the non-tax penalties can be severe. If the employer turns a blind eye, both employer and employee could end up in trouble with the tax authorities.

PERKS

The term "perks" is short for "perquisites", an old word still used in our tax laws which seems to mean a non-cash benefit. More often these days we talk of benefits in kind. By benefits in kind we usually mean benefits that are not in cash and that cannot readily be turned into cash.

The main forms of benefits in kind paid in Britain are pensions, company cars, and company share schemes. Each of these is dealt with in detail in special chapters along with related kinds of benefit. Schemes which pay people in the forms of vouchers, or other items that can readily be turned into cash are also dealt with in other chapters. In this chapter we look at any other kind of benefit. Some are caught fully by the tax laws, some in part and some not at all. This is partly a deliberate decision to treat some benefits in a favourable way, and partly because even the complexities of our modern tax system cannot find ways of catching everything!

PERKS : THE GENERAL RULE

The tax laws contain a sweeping rule aimed at bringing benefits of all kinds into the charge to income tax if they come to an employee by reason of the employment. But there are several exceptions to the rule, and also the tax is limited in some cases because the benefit does not have its full value - or, occasionally, any value.

What you cannot do, however, is accept a benefit in kind from your employer and pretend it is nothing to do with your employment. Aside from lower-paid employees, who are not caught by this rule, anything paid or provided by an employer which constitutes any kind of benefit to the employee, or to any member of the family or household of the employee, is treated as a taxable benefit provided to the employee by reason of the employment.

So wide is this rule that it has to be subject to

exceptions. Otherwise , for example, I would be taxable on the benefit of the biros I take from the stationery cupboard, or the use of the kettle in which I make my morning coffee.

THE NICS RULE

The treatment for NICs purposes of benefits in kind is completely different to that for income tax. If a benefit is a benefit in kind not convertible into cash (and leaving aside company cars and free fuel), then there is no liability to NICs on that benefit, no matter what its value.

For NICs purposes therefore, the general rule is the reverse of the income tax rule, namely there is nothing to pay. But the full width of the income tax rule means that there is usually something to pay. Even so, the absence of any charge to NICs makes the provision of benefits in kind often advantageous both to the employer and the employee. There is, after all, as much as 20% of the cost to save in this way!

UNTAXED BENEFITS

Because the very wide income tax rule is accepted, in practice, as being too wide, there are a number of exceptions to it. In each of the cases noted below, there will be no income tax (or less income tax) to pay. In each case, there will also be no NICs for the reasons just stated.

The law makes a few limited exceptions to the catch-all (or perhaps we should say tax-all) approach of the main rule. Some others are allowed by Revenue practice or concession. The list does not include things covered in the chapters on share schemes, company cars and pensions.

Employees are not taxed on accommodation,

WORKPLACE BENEFITS

supplies or services made available to them solely for work purposes. This excludes charges on, for example, computers and peripheral equipment, or equally felt pens and paper, made available at work.

WORK CANTEENS

If food is provided free or on a subsidised basis in a staff canteen, there is no tax to pay on the benefit gained through the subsidy provided that the canteen in which the meals are supplied is available to staff generally.

In practice, the tax-free provision of meals is treated more generously than this strict rule in the law and applies provided all staff have free or subsidised meals whether or not on the employer's premises.

LUNCHEON VOUCHERS

By extension, the widespread practice of giving luncheon vouchers used largely to be tax free. However, the government has for many years refused to increase the cash value of tax-free vouchers, which remains at the minimal figure of 15p a day.

STAFF PARTIES

The cost of a staff party is in principle liable to tax on each of the staff members attending the party. However, in practice the Revenue do not seek to collect tax from an employee where the cost of an annual party (whether or not at Christmas) does not exceed £50 a person.

PARKING CARS AT WORK

The provision of a free car parking space at or near work is free of extra tax (see chapter 6).

CRECHE FACILITIES

There is a restricted provision allowing employers to provide some creche facilities for children of employees without tax being charged on the employees. However, this only applies where the employer runs the scheme. The creche must also be run from non-domestic property (ie not someone's home), and the property must be provided by the employer (or another employer cooperating with that employer). The supervisors must be registered child minders.

The result of these restrictions is that workplace creches are treated as tax-free benefits, but arrangements made with independent childminders are not. Nor can an employee claim a deduction for the costs of these childminders.

Medical care or medical insurance paid for by an employer is only tax-free to the staff if the care (or insurance) is provided for overseas medical needs. If the care or insurance are provided in the United Kingdom, the employee will normally be taxed on them. There will, however, be no tax charge if the services are provided as a matter of routine by other members of the staff of the employer. For example, regular check-ups by a company doctor or attention from the company nurses will be tax-free.

MEDICAL HELP

An employee is taxable in most cases on gifts not received direct from the employer, but if the gift is in kind and not cash and is relatively small, its value will be ignored for tax purposes. For the gift to be treated as tax-free, it must cost the person giving it less than £100 together with all other gifts given to the employee by that person that year. The giver must not be connected with the employer, and the gift must not be in payment for specific services. So, for example, if someone receives a small gift from foreign visitors at the beginning or end of their visit as a matter of ceremony, it will not usually be taxed.

GIFTS FROM
THIRD PARTIES

8   Work expenses

Can you claim a tax deduction for your work expenses? Do you have a sense of humour? I hope the answer to the second question is "yes", because it isn't often the answer to the first question! Technically, you can claim some deductions, but not many and not much. In this chapter we will attempt to ensure that you get what you can claim and to explain why you can't claim other expenses.

NI CONTRIBUTIONS

First, we start with the easy if brutal rule. You cannot set any work expenses against your income for NI contribution purposes. This rule applies to all forms of expenditure, including pension contributions. There is only one exception: if you are sued by an outsider for damages. However, remember that if your employer reimburses your out of pocket expenses incurred for work reasons, that does not count as pay for NIC purposes. Both are broad rules designed to keep the system simple. They do. But simple systems do not always seem fair.

INCOME TAX

By contrast, some expenses are allowable against pay in calculating the income tax due from an employee. The underlying income tax rule is strict, and allows few expenses, although there have been a number of specific relaxations.

One reason for the strict rule is an assumption that if expenditure is needed to enable an employee to do their job, then the employer will either meet the expenditure direct, or will refund the money to the employee.

WHERE THE EMPLOYER MEETS THE COST

If the employer meets work expenditure direct, it does not count as earnings of an employee or director however high the level of earnings. However, "work expenditure" does not mean any bill incurred by or for the employee. It relates only to costs incurred, for example, in providing the employee with a workplace, tools and protective clothing. If the employee can get a personal benefit out of the expenditure, as for example with expenditure on entertainment, then the rules are even stricter on all employees except lower paid employees. In such cases, the employee gets taxed on the value of the expenditure and may only deduct the expenditure if it is within the narrow basic test for deductions, or is within one of the specific exceptions to the general rule.

The same applies where the employer refunds expenditure to the employee for work expenses that the employee met from his or her own money. If the employee is lower paid, then the money does not count as pay if it is repaying actual expenditure on work. In any other case, the employee is treated as earning the money if the general rules are met, and has to claim a deduction to avoid the tax, if this is permissible.

For example, Edwina earns £6,000 a year. She hires a taxi to take her from her workplace to another of her employer's offices, and her employer refunds the bill. That is not taxable earnings by her. Nor is it relevant to NI contributions.

However, if Edwina had earned £16,000 then strictly the refund of the taxi fare would count as earnings, subject to her right (which she would have on the facts) to claim a deduction for the expenditure equal to the amount refunded.

This process of a charge to tax followed by an equal deduction is complicated and unproductive for both employers and revenue officials. It is for this reason that ways have been found round the system, as outlined in the chapter on expense accounts.

Finally, the employee is often not incurring work expenditure personally. If, for example, you buy a new photocopy machine for your employer, you are doing so as the employer's agent. You are not personally involved in the cost, which will be met direct by the employer even though you may agree the contract. This also applies if you take money out of petty cash to rush out and buy some staples when it is discovered that the office supply has been used up. It is an example of the employer meeting the expenditure direct.

For NICs purposes, the general rule is similar to the income tax rule for the lower paid. NIC liability does not attach to a specific and distinct payment of, or contribution towards, expenses actually incurred by an employee in carrying out his or her job. However, if the payment is not "specific and distinct", then the whole of it may be regarded as earnings liable to NICs contributions by both the employer and, if the employee is liable, also the employee. For example, if the employee can be said to be making a profit out of the payment by the employer, then that element is liable to contributions. If the employer or employee cannot produce clear evidence about the extent of the profit element, then the whole payment may be caught.

WHEN THE EMPLOYER PAYS FOR TRAVEL

There are a small number of cases in which employers may pay for the costs of an employee travelling to work without the employee getting taxed on the cost:

Late night travel

If staff are required to work beyond 9 pm, and when they finish work there is either no public transport, or it would not be reasonable to expect staff to use it, employers often provide taxis or other private means of getting home. Staff taken home in this way will not be taxed on this provided that they travel home this way only occasionally (not more than 5 times a month or so), and it is neither regular nor frequent. Someone taken home in this way every day or even every Saturday might be taxed (unless lower paid).

Travel during strikes and disruption

If an employer makes special travel arrangements for staff during strikes or other times of disruption of travel, such as hiring special coaches, no tax will be imposed on employees. Nor will any tax be imposed where an employer makes payments to employees of reasonable amounts for additional expenses incurred in travel to work under these conditions. This allowance also covers the cost of overnight accommodation to avoid travel.

Severely disabled staff

Grants and social security payments may be payable to those who are severely disabled in a permanent way. There are also specific grants for those who cannot use public transport to get to and from any work they do. Those grants or equivalent help from an employer are not taxable.

Forces travel

Travel warrants or other travel provided for members of the armed forces going on leave or returning from leave is not taxable.

Offshore workers

Transport for oil workers and similar to and from offshore rigs or installations is technically taxable for anyone who is not a lower paid worker. It is, however, not taxed. Nor is related overnight accommodation.

ALLOWABLE TRAVEL

COSTS

Travel costs are allowed for income tax only if the costs are incurred for necessary travel at work. They are not allowed for NIC purposes. The costs of travel to work are never allowed for either purpose. The rules applying to cars and mileage allowances are separate and are dealt with in the special chapter on cars.

Travel at work

The cost of travel at work will normally be

allowed as an income tax deduction if the employee is required to meet the cost, and does not get a refund from the employer (or anyone else) to meet the cost. This would apply, for example, if Edwina had paid the taxi fare in the example just given but not been refunded the money by her employer.

Travel to work

The cost of travel to work is not deductible (with very rare exceptions) because it is not necessary. The fact that I live in the country and commute by rail to work, rather than live in the city near to my office so I can walk to work, is my choice. The costs of travel to work would be allowable only if I could show that the expenses I was claiming had to be incurred by everyone going to that job, and not just me. This might be met if it could be shown that the only people who could do the job would have, for example, to pay to cross a toll bridge or come on a train from a nearby station. Even then it would apply only to the necessary minimum, not the extra cost of travelling further from choice.

Groups of companies

Where someone is a director of several companies in a group, or is an employee of some and a director of others, they may be required to travel between the business locations of the different companies. Necessary travel costs travelling between the different parts of the business are deductible on the basis that it is travel at work.

There is one other general exception, though I doubt you can qualify for it. If you own a horse for the purposes of your work, then you can deduct the cost of keeping and maintaining it for work purposes against tax. This is a leftover from the days before cars (and, as we have seen, does not apply to cars). It may allow an occasional huntsman or upland shepherd to make a claim, but not many are now able to claim!

THE BASIC EXPENSES DEDUCTION RULES

The general rules for allowing deduction of expenses against income for income tax purposes is strict. **Expenditure can only be allowed under the general rule if**

It is revenue expenditure not capital

The goods or services are necessary for the job, and

The expenditure is made wholly and exclusively for the purposes of the job.

Expenditure on capital items (for example, a computer bought for the job) may possibly qualify under other kinds of allowances, known as capital allowances, but does not qualify under the general rules.

The effect of these rules is to block a claim for expenditure unless the person claiming the deduction can prove that anyone having to do that employee's job would have to pay out that expenditure. Otherwise it is not necessary.

In addition, the employee has to show that the whole of the expenditure was for work reasons. If part of it is for something else, then the test is failed.

Finally, the employee must show that the only reason for the expenditure is the job. Again, if the employee has a number of reasons for the expenditure, only some of which relate to the job, then the tests have been failed, and the employee gets no deduction. These rules have long been criticised as harsh. In practice, this has been recognised by granting a small number of exceptions to the rule. For example, professional employees having to pay subscriptions to their professional bodies are allowed to make a deduction, and workmen are allowed a small deduction to meet the cost of clothes and tools.

The cost of a capital purchase, such as a car or a computer, cannot be set off against income direct, whatever the reason for its purchase. The only deductions or allowances for the cost of capital items are special *capital allowances*.

CAPITAL ITEMS

Employees can only claim capital allowances if they can show that it is necessary for them to buy capital equipment for their work where the equipment has a life of several years, and is not used up within a year or two of buying it. It will cover a car or boat, a computer or textbooks. But journals or computer peripherals are revenue expenditure.

However, in practice an employee is rarely entitled to claim capital allowances because it is difficult to show that the cost of the equipment is necessary for the work. With rare exceptions, the employer will buy or finance necessary capital equipment. For example, if you are expected to use a computer at work, then the Revenue would expect your employer to provide it. It is not enough that you want an extra computer (say, a portable). You have to show not only that you could not do the job without the computer, but that no one could. That is a tough test, and it is meant to be a tough text.

It may be that if your job is a skilled one, you need certain tools and reference books which your employer does not supply, but that you need. Allowances are made for tools for some employees - see the note below.

CAPITAL ALLOWANCES

The only kind of capital expenditure for which people can claim tax allowances in connection with their work is money spent on what is officially called *plant and machinery*. In practice this covers the range of expense on equipment bought by someone in connection with work or business. It covers cars and other forms of vehicle. There are special rules applying to cars, and these are described in the chapter on cars. While dealing with means of travel at work, it even covers horses!

More generally, allowances may apply to any kind of equipment that is used for a job, whether it is a power or hand tool, right the way through to books and manuals and filofaxes or similar personal organisers. (I have always found that organisers only work for those who are organised anyway. Those who are not organised get little advantage from a personal organiser. On that basis, it could be said that these little devices are never necessary!)

To be allowable against earnings from an employment, the employee must show that the equipment is necessary for use in the performance of the duties of the employment. It must also be shown, to claim a full allowance, that the expense was wholly and exclusively for use in the performance of the duties, and that the employee owns the equipment at least at some point during the period of claim for the allowance.

WHAT IS ALLOWABLE?

The next part of the chapter is an alphabetical list of items with a discussion of whether they are deductible against income tax - and if so, how. Remember that the list leaves out NICs in nearly every case because the general rule is that no deduction is allowed for that purpose.

Agents

Some groups of workers are treated by the Revenue as employees even though in other ways they work as if they were self-employed. This is particularly true of many actors, singers, musicians, dancers and other theatrical artists. All these groups of people may find employment through agents and agencies, and they have to pay the agencies' fees from their salaries. Fees paid to licensed agencies and paid by the entertainer out of her or his pay are deductible against income tax if the fees are a percentage of that pay. Entertainers may also claim a deduction for the VAT payable on the fee. The maximum amount deductible is 17.5% of pay.

Babysitting and nursery expenses

Expenses you pay for these services are never allowable. Employers can make some facilities available without you having to pay tax on them, and those on social security benefits are being allowed to earn some money to meet these expenses without losing benefit, but those are the only people helped in this way.

Books and journals

Buying *newspapers and magazines* is often regarded by people as part of their job, but the Revenue will rarely allow a deduction for the cost. They would only be allowable if anyone doing the job had to buy those newspapers. For example, news reporters buying rival newspapers for ideas or to watch the opposition will not be allowed to deduct the cost because they don't have to read other papers - at least in the view of the courts. Some journals are provided in return for *professional subscriptions*, and these may be allowed - see below. Buying books is not regarded as revenue expenditure but capital expenditure, so these costs fall outside the general rules. However, if the books are necessary (as certain manuals and guides may be), then a claim for a *capital allowance* can be made. This is because books are regarded as "plant and machinery"!

Clothing

The general rule is that the cost of clothes bought to wear at work is not deductible. The cost of special clothing (for example a uniform) would be allowable if the employee has to wear it, but the employer does not provide it or pay for it. In many cases allowances have been agreed with the trade unions to take care of this, for example in the case of craftsmen and women or industrial labourers. See **Tools** below.

Computers and computer peripherals

Unless the equipment is necessary, no allowance is possible. An allowance for a computer would be a capital allowance, but the Revenue is likely to need a lot of convincing before agreeing that the computer is bought for necessary work reasons. And if it is, then it cannot also be used for other purposes. So, a computer at home that is loaded up with the children's games cannot be said to be wholly for work purposes!

Educational courses (see also **Training courses** below)

The rules also apply to further education courses, but will not apply to general academic qualifications such as A-levels or part-time degrees.

Employing others to help with your work

This is not deductible in any usual case of employment. For example, if I agree to pay my wife or friend to help me do my job, I cannot deduct the payments I make to her (or him) from my own earnings. This is because it will not be necessary for me to sub-contract my job in this way. If I am able to do this without the employer being able to stop it, then I am probably not an employee at all, but a self-employed person. One of the key aspects of being an employee is a personal obligation to provide services. They cannot be passed on to anyone else. Unless it is necessary for this to be done, no allowance is possible. Therefore I will not be allowed to deduct the cost of doing so, even though my employee might be liable to tax on the earnings. This prevents employees employing their wives or husbands so as to share out income between them in the way that many self-employed couples do.

Glasses and medical appliances

If equipment is needed for safety purposes, it is the duty of the employer to provide it under health and safety legislation. The Revenue therefore take the view that it is not necessary for employees to buy it. Items such as ordinary glasses that people need for work are not deductible. This is because, although they may be necessary for the individual, they are not necessary for the job.

Income tax

Employees cannot deduct their income tax as an expense against earnings for income tax purposes (or NIC purposes). Nor are NIC contributions deductible. This ban also covers any costs on professional fees (for example to an accountant) for sorting out your tax liability.

Insurance

Employees who take out their own private health insurance or insurance against loss of pay because of sickness cannot claim tax relief for the premiums. There is a general relief for private health insurance for all those aged 60 or over, and older employees will be able to take advantage of this. The various providers of private health insurance will provide full details. Benefits received from health insurance contracts, or from income replacement policies providing short-term benefits lasting no more than a year, will not be taxed.

Meals at work

You cannot deduct the cost of meals at work, even if you work not only away from home but also away from your usual place of work. However, if your employer subsidises a canteen, the benefit is not taxable.

NI contributions

See **income tax** above.

Pension contributions

Contributions to occupational and personal pensions are usually deductible in full. See the chapter on pensions.

Professional subscriptions

Most annual professional subscriptions are deductible under statutory authority. Fees paid by employed professionals to remain on professional registers, such as the practising fees paid by architects, dentists, opticians, patent agents and solicitors, are deductible in full. So are fees paid to associations and organisations set up on a non-profit basis to help professionals (provided they are not confined to a local area). The Revenue is empowered to approve individual associations for relief on this basis, and maintains a list of the organisations it has approved.

If you belong, or are considering joining, any of these organisations, then check if tax relief is available. Subscriptions often include the price of a regular journal or magazine. In some cases an extra subscription to the journal has to be paid, but this may be allowed as in effect part of the subscription. Organisations not currently approved may also apply to be added to the list of approved bodies.

Public sector posts

The Treasury has power to authorise set deductions from income tax for work expenses for any group of employees or office holders paid out of public funds. These are notified to those concerned. MPs are not taxed on their expense allowances for travel from home either to the House of Commons or their constituencies.

Security costs

Where employees run special security risks by reason of their work, then the extra costs of protecting them may technically count as income. If that happens, a deduction against income tax to cover the cost will be allowable if the conditions are met. The main condition is that there is a special threat to the personal security of the individual.

Telephones

Technically, if you have a telephone at home for work reasons the cost is only deductible if the telephone is necessary for the job, and you use it for no other purpose. If you have two telephones at home (perhaps one for an office fax), then you may be able to show this. Otherwise you are unlikely to be able to claim a deduction under the strict rules, except for the individual costs of business calls. In practice, you may be able to agree an apportionment of the total cost with the local tax office. These rules will apply whether or not your employer makes a contribution to the cost of you having a phone at home - except that the contribution is taxable.

Mobile phones raise the same issues. If the employer provides the mobile phone with the job, there is a tax charge. The use of the phone is treated as a benefit worth £200 for tax reasons unless the holder uses it only for business purposes, or refunds to the employer the full cost of any private use.

Tools

The Revenue have agreed a long list of flat rate deductions for employees in many kinds of activity. This is meant as an average deduction to cover the tools necessary for the job, and any special clothing that is also necessary. It is based on the assumption that uniforms and safety equipment needed for a job will be supplied by the employers, but also recognises that this does not meet all necessary costs. The figures have been negotiated with trades unions. The list covers both craftsmen (and women) and labourers in the agricultural and forestry, metals (including mining and precious metals), building and construction (including building materials), clothing and textiles, electrical and electricity supply, engineering, food, glass, heating (including gas supply), mining and quarrying, printing (including textile printing), transport (railways, sea and public transport), wood and furniture, and leather industries. They also cover uniformed bank staff, police officers and prison officers. The allowances are usually modest, ranging from a yearly amount of £20 to £90, but some (for example aluminium workers) get higher allowances. If you work in any of these areas, you should check for any allowance with your trade union, or check details through the local tax office.

These allowances are generally granted to those within the approved lists without further question. However, they do not prevent someone claiming a larger amount if they can justify it. Justifying it will in practice not be easy.

Training courses and tuition

If it can be shown that an employee is required to attend a course because of the job, and the employee has personally to bear the expense, then it could be claimed as a deduction. However, attending courses just to make you better at your job, or in order to gain promotion, is not necessary in this sense, and you cannot therefore claim a deduction for the cost. There are also two more specific provisions for a tax relief.

If a course of training counts or is capable of counting for an NVQ (National Vocational Qualification) or its Scottish equivalent then the fees spent on attending the course, or being assessed as competent as a result of the course, can be claimed as a deduction against income tax. However, this only applies to those who have left school and are not receiving any other public help to meet that cost. The course must be undertaken personally, and must be for work rather than leisure or recreational reasons. In some cases, the tax relief can be built into the fee, in which case, of course, it cannot be claimed twice.

The Revenue have also slightly relaxed the general rules preventing employees claiming a deduction for fees for attending a training course (and for essential books), but only where all the following conditions are met :

You are allowed time off during normal hours to attend

Your employer either requires or encourages you to attend the course to make you better at your job

You have to attend the course on all or most days for at least 4 weeks on a full-time basis

In addition, courses must be in the UK, but it does not matter whether the course leads to a qualification. The rules under which employers can refund costs to employees for attending courses without the employees being charged tax on the refund are much broader.

Travel costs
See **Cars, p.130**

Uniforms
See **Clothing** above

Use of home as office
The increase in telecottages and telecommuting means that more employees, as well as the self-employed, are working at home. In these cases, employers may make allowances towards home expenses or equipment used at home. These may be treated as earnings, leaving the employee to claim a deduction. An employee will be allowed a deduction for costs incurred (or to

offset against an employer's payment) in connection with working at home only if the usual strict tests are met. Expenses would have to be shown as necessary - those which anyone working at home has to meet. It will be hard to show, for example, that the heating and lighting is spent in this way, because these costs are shared throughout the house, and claims of this kind will not be allowed.

9   *Pensions*

Whether you do it at 65, 60, 70 or 50, at some point you will retire. And whether you call it a pension, deferred pay, savings, or income support you will need money to replace your earnings.

Most people have a pension to take over when their earnings end. That is not only wise when looking to the future, it is also one of the best ways now of saving in a way that keeps your present tax bill down. However, the tax system probably also shapes your pension entitlement. This is because the tax privileges granted to pensions and pension funds are subject to limits and conditions. Your pension rights are also shaped by the National Insurance system. In this chapter we look at both - at what you pay and get now, and what you get and pay later.

PAYING FOR A PENSION

You may, or may not, be paying for a pension as you work. If you earn enough to pay NI contributions, then you are probably paying for a pension: the state retirement pension.

You may also be paying contributions to your employer's pension scheme - or you may be in a job under which contributions are paid by your employer for you, but you do not have to contribute. If so, you will in due course be entitled to an occupational pension.

In addition, or instead, you may have your own private pension arrangements, for which you pay (and your employer may also contribute).

NICS, PENSIONS AND INCOME TAX

If you pay NICs, then these do not count for income tax purposes. You pay the income tax and the NICs separately and in full. However, if you pay contributions towards an occupational pension or private pension of a kind approved by the tax authorities, your contributions are deductible against tax. So you will save the tax you would otherwise pay on the earnings you use on your contributions. Further, you may pay a lower level of NICs because you are paying the other premiums.

We must also look at what you get from each kind of pension. First, we examine the pension that all except the lowest earners pay for - the state retirement pension.

Retirement Age

At what age do you have to retire? Although most people believe this to be 65 or 60, the official answer is that there is no such thing as a compulsory retirement age.

Individual employment contracts may make you retire from that job at a set age (often 65, but sometimes as low as 45). But there is nothing stopping you taking another job at that time. By law, the age must be the same for women and men.

The state retirement age is 65 for men and 60 for women. The age for women is increasing to 65 in twenty years' time. You may claim any entitlement to a state retirement pension at that age, and you stop having to pay NI contributions. However, you may delay your claim to a state pension for up to 5 years if you wish without further contribution.

If you have an occupational pension, the pension scheme will also have a retirement age - that is, the age when you can claim a pension. This varies between schemes. In addition, a growing number of schemes allow for early retirement, although they reduce pension entitlement for early claims.

Below the standard retirement age there is often provision for early retirement on medical grounds. Special rules apply to this.

PAYING FOR A
STATE PENSION

That is where the employees' NI contributions go. Most of the contributions paid by employees and their employers are paid into the National Insurance Fund. The chief purpose of that fund is to pay for state retirement pensions. So, are you paying for your pension that way? Yes and no.

You are paying for your own future pension entitlement because it will be based on the total of contributions you have paid. But the state will not save up your contributions in the way private pension funds do. Instead, it will use the cash you pay in to pay out to today's pensioners. It is a pay as you go (or possibly pay as they get) system. It therefore works by giving you a pension at the announced annual rate based on your contribution record.

You are liable to start paying contributions when you are 16, and to pay them until you reach the state retirement age. At present, that is 65 for men and 60 for women, but by 2020 the retirement age for women will have been increased to 65 to be the same as men. Of course, you can retire below that age, but you will not be entitled to claim a pension until then, and you may remain liable to pay contributions (or lose pension entitlement if you allow a gap to be created).

YOUR
CONTRIBUTION RECORD

Every time you pay an employee's NI contribution, the amount is recorded. Over the weeks and months of each year, your record is accumulated - though you do not see this on your pay slip. For example, if you are paid weekly, your employer must apply the modified form of PAYE for NI contributions to your pay each week. If you earn over the lower earnings level for that week, you pay a NI contribution. If not, you pay nothing. As your contribution is a percentage of your earnings, the more you earn in the week, the more you pay.

If you have earned over the lower earnings limit each week throughout the year, you will have a contribution recorded for each week worked. That contribution will count for you in two ways.

YOUR TWO STATE PENSIONS

You are first entitled, if you pay enough contributions, to the basic flat-rate state retirement pension. This is payable weekly to all those who are over state retirement age and who have retired from work. In 1995/96, the basic pension is £58.85 a week.

You are also entitled to a SERPS pension - a state earnings-related pension scheme. This pension is based on your lifetime total of earnings-related contributions.

However, if you have a job which is contracted-out, then you will not get the SERPS pension. Instead, you will pay a lower NI contribution. You can only be contracted-out if you are contributing towards either an occupational pension (organised by your employer) or a personal pension (usually organised by you).

In each case, your entitlement depends on what you have paid. If you do not contribute, you do not benefit. Because the basic contributions are compulsory, and are collected by employers, employees normally have good contribution records, at least they do if they have worked continuously and have earned enough to be paying contributions.

What happens if you did not earn every week? You will only have a complete record if your earnings add up to more than the equivalent of the lower earnings level for every week.

KATH PAYS TOO LITTLE

For example, Kath has a job for 40 week during the year, and earns £70 for each week of work. In the other 12 weeks she earns nothing. Her total earnings, on which she pays NICs, is £2,800. This is the equivalent of a little under £54 a week for the full 52 weeks of the year. If the lower earnings limit for the year is less than £54, then Kath will not have a full year's contributions. (In 1995/96, the lower earnings limit is £58, so her record is deficient.)

Where the contributions for a year fall below the lower earnings limit, they do not qualify as a contributing year towards pension entitlement. This may or may not be important to Kath. And it may or may not be avoidable.

Whether Kath has or has not paid enough to count her contributions toward her pension depends on whether she will have enough years that do qualify. If it is important, how is it avoidable? It may be that Kath had other earnings on which contributions were not paid - for example, benefits in kind. If so, the short-term saving may prove quite expensive in the long term, possibly very expensive.

Had Kath earned much more during her work, she would not have had a problem. For example, the following year she gets a new job at £250 a week. But it only lasts 20 weeks. What is her position that year ?

Kath pays contributions on the full £250 in each of the 20 weeks, a total of £5,000. Averaged over 52 weeks, this is just under £100 a week, and well over the lower earnings limit. She therefore has a full contribution record for the year.

Kath can only claim a full state retirement pension if she has a full contribution year for most years of her working life. Kath left school at 16, and worked most years. She will retire shortly at 60, the state retirement age for women.

ADDING UP THE YEARS

To claim a full basic pension, Kath will have had to have paid enough contributions to have a qualifying year for nine out of ten years for each year she worked or could have worked from 16 to 60.

This is a total of 44 years. So, Kath is allowed to have four, but only four, years which do not qualify for contribution purposes. She must have a good contribution record for 40 years to meet the test.

IF THE YEARS DO NOT ADD UP

What if Kath had stayed at school to 18, then worked for a few years but, after marrying, took several years off to have children, and only went back to work after that. She took a further two years off when her husband was posted abroad (although she worked overseas), and she has had a patchy career since, as we have seen.

This kind of record is typical of many women, and is increasingly typical of men too. Do they all lose pension as a result? Kath may do so, but we need to look carefully at each stage of her career to see the full picture. Even then, if her record is short of contributions, she may be able to pay some extra contributions to patch up her record.

CONTRIBUTION CREDITS

First, Kath will be entitled to contribution credits for some periods of her life. Contribution credits are deemed or notional contributions. They are payable for a variety of reasons.

In Kath's case, she may have had contributions credited for several reasons. Firstly, all those who stay on in education after 16 are entitled to credits while at school. Kath only starts work at 18, and will be regarded as having paid contributions until then.

Second, if during her life Kath received any of the contributory benefits, she will have been regarded as having paid contributions while receiving the benefits. This will apply if she received sickness benefit (but not statutory sick pay from an employer) or the state maternity benefit (but not maternity pay from her employer) or unemployment benefit (but not income support) if she claimed after losing a job. Any of these may cover other gaps in her career.

Next, as a mum, Kath is entitled to claim home responsibilities protection for the time she was home looking after the children. If she was covered by this, she can leave those years out of her working life. For example, if Kath qualified for the HRP for five years while her two children were born, then she can leave those years out of the years counting towards her pension. Her working life is then shortened from 44 years to 39 (with three, not four, years "spare").

If you have gaps in your contribution record, the following kinds of credits may be available to supplement your actual contributions with notional contributions :

CREDITS

For the year in which you are 16 and the next two years

For men who reach their 60th birthday and the next four years, and are not contributing

For periods on full time training courses

For periods of unemployment

For periods of sickness or disability

For women for any maternity pay period

For anyone on jury service who is not contributing

For anyone receiving invalid care allowance

You can also get home responsibility protection to reduce the period you have to work in order to qualify for a pension. You may be able to get this if you stay at home to look after children, or elderly or sick people (unless you are getting invalid care allowance credits already).

If you were married, and did not have a full contribution record during the marriage, you may be able to claim credits from the contributions paid by your former wife or husband. This applies after a divorce or death.

All these credits and provisions will fill many of the gaps in Kath's contribution record, but there is still more to come.

PAYING OVERSEAS

For work purposes, your home base is not Britain (or Northern Ireland, which has a separate social security system), it is the whole of the European Union, and some more : Austria, Belgium, Denmark, Finland, France, Germany, Greece, Ireland, Italy, Luxembourg, Netherlands, Portugal, Spain, and Sweden (which form, with the United Kingdom, the European Union) and Iceland, Liechtenstein and Norway (which form, with the EU, the European Economic Area). If you work in any of those areas, any social security contributions you pay in those states count automatically toward your pension entitlement in the UK. Or should, if the procedure works right. That is your entitlement under EU law which applies automatically in the UK.

To stop small periods overseas creating gaps in a contribution record, you remain liable to the British social security system (and contributions) for up to 52 weeks after stopping work in the UK.

Once over that period, you will become liable to pay under the system where you are working, but it still counts towards a British pension.

There are several other countries which also have agreements with Britain under which your contributions overseas count here. For full details you should contact your local social security office and ask for their detailed leaflets in the "SA" series about the countries that concern you.

In Kate's case, we do not know where she and her husband went, but there's a fair chance that it was one of the countries covered by either the EU and EEA or one of the international social security agreements. If it was, then she may have contributions to fill yet more of the gaps.

MAKING UP THE GAPS

Even then, Kate may not have got her record up to the point where only three years are missing. If she has, then she has a full record. If not, she might think it worth her while to buy extra contributions to fill the gaps. She could also fill the gaps with any contributions she has paid as a self-employed individual. (For details of self-employed contributions, see the companion book *Don't Pay Too Much Tax if You're Self-Employed*).

How does she do this? By buying voluntary contributions (technically known as Class 3 contributions). You can do this for any period in which you are not paying either employee's contributions or contributions as a self-employed person to a high enough level to meet the contribution requirements.

VOLUNTARY
CONTRIBUTIONS

These cost just a little less than the self-employed flat-rate (class 2) contributions for a week, adding up to a sum in the region of £300 for a full year in recent years.

They can be paid by those living in the UK, or assumed to be living here, for a year when other contributions are not enough. They can be paid at the end of that year, or for up to six years after the year. (This may perhaps be longer if there have been genuine and understandable mistakes on your part, for example because you were given wrong information by your employer and had no reason to realise this at the time.)

To find out if you can pay voluntary contributions, and how much these will be, you need to ask your local social security office for what is often called a deficiency statement. This is issued by the Contributions Agency on request, and tells you whether there is any shortfall in your contribution record.

Paying these contributions may be useful, for instance, if you decide to take a year off from work, and so pay no contributions at all, but also are not entitled to receive any credits for sickness or unemployment.

HER HUSBAND'S
CONTRIBUTIONS

There is one other way Kate might gain a better

contribution record. This occurs, however, only if she gets divorced or if her husband dies. If her husband had a better contribution record than she did during the period of their marriage, she can claim a personal state pension entitlement on the basis of her husband's contributions, provided that she was not claiming entitlement to the women's reduced rate of contributions.

The entitlement to "borrow" the former husband's contributions also applies to a man who wishes to borrow his former wife's contributions. It does not apply to unmarried couples.

This entitlement to rely on the contributions of the former husband or wife reflects the fact that the social security system offers additional pension to a retired person for their spouse, and also widow's (and widower's) benefits.

Some women are entitled to pay employee's contributions at a reduced rate (currently 3.85% of their earnings). This only applies to women who were married in 1977, and have not since been widowed or divorced. They had the right to elect for the reduced rate at that time, but the right was withdrawn that year. It is lost when someone is divorced or when the husband dies. It can also be given up voluntarily.

THE WOMEN'S
REDUCED RATE

When a woman pays at the reduced rate, she usually saves on NI contributions, but in return she loses all rights to the contributory benefits - particularly a separate entitlement to state pension. (She may instead be entitled to a pension through her husband when he reaches retirement age).

Is it worth staying on the reduced rate? This will

depend on personal circumstances. It is not worth it to women earning just above the earnings limit or who will get no real benefit from the extra contributions (because of other pension entitlements of their own or their husbands), but it is worth it to women who would not get any other pension entitlement in any event.

A woman who has opted for the reduced rate cannot claim home responsibility protection or pay voluntary contributions while the reduced rate option stands, and these ought also to be borne in mind.

ARE PENSIONS TAXABLE?

For income tax purposes, pensions are treated in the same way as earnings, so you are liable to income tax on them. This is true both of your state retirement pension and any occupational or private pension.

The only difference of significance for pensioners is that those over 65 are entitled to a larger personal allowance (see chapter 2). In effect, this means that a person receiving only the basic state retirement pension will not pay tax. But if someone receives SERPS or another pension as well, the two are added together, and tax applied to the amount that exceeds the allowance. This will be done by PAYE in the same way as for earnings. Tax is never deducted from the state retirement pension.

SERPS

You cannot make up the gaps for a SERPS pension. This depends entirely on the total of employee's contributions you pay.

The exact entitlement to weekly SERPS pension

depends on the annual totals of NIC contributions as an employee over the whole career of the contributor.

Each year, the total of NI contributions paid by the employee is added up. Those of the employer do not count. The employee's total is recorded in the Contribution Agency's central records (maintained at Newcastle upon Tyne).

In order to stop the value of the contributions in any year being eroded by inflation, the amount for a year is adjusted by an earnings factor to increase its value to take account of cumulative inflation between the year in which the contributions were paid and the year in which any entitlement to pension is worked out. Earnings factors are officially announced each year for all earlier years.

The lifetime total of contributions, with each year separately adjusted for inflation by the correct earnings factor, is worked out when a claim to SERPS is made.

The maximum SERPS is payable to someone who has paid the maximum employee's contributions for each working year since 1978 continuing throughout a full working life, and whose job is not, and has not been, contracted-out.

HOW BIG IS A SERPS?

The entitlement is worked out on the basis of the total of contributions paid. In each year, that total is added up. The amount equal to the year's basic contributions are deducted from this.

The year's basic contributions are worked out assuming that the employee earns exactly the lower earnings level during each week of the year. For example, if the employee earns £70 each week, and the lower earnings limit in that year is £50, the total contribution each week for SERPS purposes is £20. This is because the other £50 is paying for the basic flat-rate pension.

A total amount of contributions for each year is worked out in this way. At the end of the year, the total is revised by reference to that year's earnings factor to take account of inflation. It takes full records (and, in practice, a computer) to arrive at this total, and not many employees are in a position to check it!

Once the Contributions Agency has established the total, pension is payable weekly on an annual amount of 1.25% of the total contributions. For instance, if someone earns £100 more than the lower earnings level this year, this year's total is £5,200. If the contributor has earned the cash equivalent of that for 15 years, they have a notional total earnings of £78,000. This will give an annual figure of just under £1,000, or about £40 a week. (If we assume the contributions have always been at 10% for simplicity, the total contributions for SERPS will be about £7,800 during that period.)

GOOD NEWS, BAD NEWS

The entitlement of those now retiring to SERPS is good news. The bad news is for those some years from retirement. There is no way that the state can go on paying SERPS at that generous level. If it did, the NI Fund would in due course go bust. Why? Because far more of us are living longer in retirement, and the younger ones among us are having fewer children. The result is fewer people paying contributions and more people claiming pensions for longer. This problem starts to get very serious next century.

To stop things getting out of control the amount of pension that is earned by contributions starts going down in 1999 and becomes 1% (rather than 1.25%) by 2009. At the same time, the real values of both the lower earnings limit and the upper earnings limit as earnings are going down each year. This is because they are increased each year by reference to increases in prices that year, not increases in earnings. In nearly every recent year, average earnings have increased more than average prices.

Without getting too technical, the result is that the real level of the state pension, as compared with average earnings, decreases every year. What is more, it has been doing so for several years past as well.

SERPS therefore only takes into account earnings in any earnings period up to the maximum earnings relevant to employees' NI contributions. At any one time, this is roughly one and a half times the average earnings for the period. Anyone who in any period (and for any reason, such as a bonus) earns more than that does not earn extra SERPS entitlement.

In practice, many who might claim the maximum SERPS do not do so because they have other pension arrangements. These are the people who have other pension arrangements and are contracted-out of the state scheme.

CONTRACTING-OUT

A main reason for contracting-out is that those with better earnings can get a better deal out of occupational or private arrangements than out of the state scheme. As part of this deal, they pay lower NI contributions, although those who have contracted out with a private arrangement still pay at the higher rate and then have the difference rebated to the pension provider by the DSS.

Both you and your employer can decide to contract-out of the state pension scheme - though you cannot contract out of the basic retirement pension. Your employer can decide to set up an approved occupational pension scheme for either all the staff working for the employer or some groups of those staff.

When the employer gets approval for the scheme, it can be opted out. Anyone joining that scheme must pay the contributions to that scheme (as must the employer) but pays the reduced contracted-out NI contributions.

TAKING THE RIGHT DECISION

All employees now have the right to opt out of an occupational pension scheme as well. Their choice is to pay instead into a personal pension, or to opt out of pension provision schemes altogether. Many people have changed from an occupational pension scheme to personal pensions - some, but not all, of them wisely and sensibly. For some the decision to opt out has been an expensive mistake.

It is impossible in this short book to discuss in detail when it is better for someone to stay in their occupational pension scheme, and when it is better to opt out, but I must add a clear word of warning. While for some people personal pensions are an excellent idea, for others private schemes are less good than their employer's schemes. If you want to consider what you should do, get full details of your employer's scheme and then get professional advice on the alternatives. And do not take a decision until you have thought through that advice.

For example, one of the factors that may influence your decision is your likely career pattern. Are you going to stay with the same employer, or are you going to move around (possibly to other countries). You have some rights to move your pension from one employer to another, but this may sometimes not be as advantageous as a personal pension, which can be moved.

Whatever is the right choice in terms of sorts of pension, opting out of both the state scheme and alternative private schemes is even less of a good idea. In fact, unless you know you have alternative sources of income available, it is not a good idea at all. In that kind of case you would be entitled only to the basic state pension and you will otherwise be relying on the means-tested benefits such as income support and housing benefit. You are also losing the generous tax advantages given to all forms of pension.

OCCUPATIONAL PENSIONS

Why is it such a good idea to save through a pension scheme? The answer lies in the way the tax system favours pension arrangements of an approved kind.

First, when you pay your pension contribution, you can claim a tax deduction for it. Put another way, if the pension contribution is £100, it will only cost you £75 actual lost earnings (£60 at the 40 per cent tax rate).

Second, you do not get taxed on your employer's contributions. In many schemes, the employer is paying over 10 per cent of your earnings into the pension scheme as the employer's premium. In some cases that figure is 20 per cent or more. Yet, this is not treated as your earnings for tax purposes.

Better still, once your money has gone into the pension scheme, it earns income (and gains in capital value) without any tax at all. If you were to save your money direct, and seek to earn profits on the stock exchange, you would find it difficult to make anything approaching the profits after tax that a pension fund can make. This is because only a few of the forms of saving that you can use are tax-free for the levels of savings required for a reasonable pension. So some of your savings will have built up for many years free of tax.

It is only when you claim the pension that you pay tax. And even then, you can claim a lump sum as part of your pension which is tax free. That is why there are few better ways of paying less tax than saving through an approved pension scheme. But what do you get for your contributions (apart from reduced tax bills)?

PENSION ENTITLEMENTS

Your pension rights are determined by the scheme set up by your employer, or, in the case of personal pensions, by the scheme for the pension and the contract you agree with the pension provider.

The precise entitlement of employees varies from one scheme to another, but the Revenue have put maximum levels on pension entitlement - and a small forest of other conditions. If a pension scheme is to get tax approval, it must meet these conditions. In practice therefore, most people will find that their pensions are limited by the tax conditions.

The main tax conditions are :

No pension before 50 (although it is usually higher)

Full pension only after at least 10 years

membership of the scheme (but most schemes demand 30 or 40 years for full entitlement)

A maximum pension of 2/3rd of final salary (that is, of earnings in the year of retirement)

A ceiling of maximum earnings on which pension entitlement can be earned. The figure is adjusted from year to year and is currently about £80,000.

A maximum tax free lump sum of 1 1/2 times final salary (but limited by the maximum salary figure).

As noted, schemes are not often as generous as this. More typical is a scheme which grants a retirement pension equal to half the employee's earnings just before retirement, if contributions have been paid over a working life of at least 30 years, and often 40 years.

The traditional scheme is one that entitles the employee to a specific benefit on retirement. However, pensions may be based instead on what are termed money purchase schemes.

In these schemes you pay in a contribution each year at a given level. These contributions are saved up. The savings are then used to pay a pension to you on retirement. How much pension will depend on how well your savings have done, and how much income can be earned by them. It is impossible to tell what that level will be many years ahead, although some intelligent guesses can be made. However, the advantage is that these schemes are financially secure, and will always meet the obligations on them (if, that is, they are run properly).

PERSONAL PENSIONS

Personal pensions are usually money purchase pensions. The important figure here is the maximum amount that an individual can pay in and get tax relief. The figures are quite generous. This is because they are designed to allow an employee to pay in similar sums to those paid in by employees and employers together.

The current maximum depends on your age. The figures are:

Your age (at beginning of tax year)	Maximum contribution
Under 36	17.5%
36-45	20.0%
46-50	25.0%
51-55	30.0%
56-60	35.0%
Over 60	40.0%

The percentage figure is the amount of your earnings that can be paid into the fund while still claiming tax relief. It is also limited by the maximum annual figure. If your pay is pensionable by some other scheme, then it does not count for these purposes. You cannot claim two sets of tax relief for pensions on the same earnings.

AVCs

What you can do sometimes is top up your occupational pension with additional voluntary contributions (AVCs), and claim tax relief on these. Those who run your occupational pension scheme should give you advice about this. They allow you to increase the amount of pension you can get in a tax-privileged way. But you cannot use them to get more out of a pension than the Revenue's limits.

Index